Self-~~Love~~

Unlock Your Potential with Self-Compassion, Radical Acceptance, and Unshakeable Confidence

VitalSpark Synergy

© Copyright 2024 - All rights reserved.

The content contained within this book may not be reproduced, duplicated or transmitted without direct written permission from the author or the publisher.

Under no circumstances will any blame or legal responsibility be held against the publisher, or author, for any damages, reparation, or monetary loss due to the information contained within this book, either directly or indirectly.

Legal Notice:

This book is copyright protected. It is only for personal use. You cannot amend, distribute, sell, use, quote or paraphrase any part, or the content within this book, without the consent of the author or publisher.

Disclaimer Notice:

Please note the information contained within this document is for educational and entertainment purposes only. All effort has been executed to present accurate, up to date, reliable, complete information. No warranties of any kind are declared or implied. Readers acknowledge that the author is not engaged in the rendering of legal, financial, medical or professional advice. The content within this book has been derived from various sources. Please consult a licensed professional before attempting any techniques outlined in this book.

By reading this document, the reader agrees that under no circumstances is the author responsible for any losses, direct or indirect, that are incurred as a result of the use of the information contained within this document, including, but not limited to, errors, omissions, or inaccuracies.

Table of Contents

INTRODUCTION 1

CHAPTER 1: UNDERSTANDING SELF-LOVE 5

    THE BASICS OF SELF-LOVE 5
        Breaking Free From Negative Messages 5
        Seeking Support on Your Self-Love Journey 6
        Celebrating Your Strengths and Successes 6
    SELF-LOVE ISN'T SELFISH 7
        Incorporating Self-Love Into Your Daily Life 7
        The Lifelong Practice of Self-Love 8
        Your Self-Love Challenge 8
        The Ripple Effect of Self-Love 9
    THE MOST IMPORTANT JOB YOU'LL EVER HAVE 10
    OVERCOMING OBSTACLES ON YOUR SELF-LOVE JOURNEY 10
    THE BEAUTY OF IMPERFECTION 11
    THE GIFT OF SELF-LOVE 12
    CASE STUDY: SARAH'S SELF-LOVE JOURNEY 12
    CULTIVATING A GROWTH MINDSET 13
    FINDING YOUR SELF-LOVE TRIBE 15
    EXERCISE 1: SELF-LOVE AFFIRMATION PRACTICE 17
    EXERCISE 2: MIRROR WORK 18
    SELF-REFLECTION QUESTIONS 19

CHAPTER 2: OVERCOMING BARRIERS TO SELF-LOVE 23

    LETTING GO OF NEGATIVE SELF-TALK 24
    LETTING GO OF PERFECTIONISM 25
    RELEASING TOXIC RELATIONSHIPS 25
    OVERCOMING THE FEAR OF JUDGMENT 26
    LETTING GO OF SELF-DOUBT 27
    HEALING FROM PAST MISTAKES 28
    LETTING GO OF THE FEAR OF FAILURE 29
    CULTIVATING SELF-TRUST AND INNER WISDOM 29
    EMBRACING VULNERABILITY AND AUTHENTIC CONNECTION 31
    EMBRACING THE JOURNEY 33
    CASE STUDY: OVERCOMING PERFECTIONISM AND EMBRACING AUTHENTICITY 34
    EXERCISE 1: REFRAMING NEGATIVE SELF-TALK 35
    EXERCISE 2: EMBRACING IMPERFECTION THROUGH CREATIVE SELF-EXPRESSION 36
    SELF-REFLECTION QUESTIONS 38
    YOUR FEEDBACK MATTERS! 39

CHAPTER 3: BEGIN YOUR PATH TO SELF-LOVE 41
- Embracing Your Authentic Self 41
- Self-Acceptance: Embracing Your Flaws 42
- Self-Esteem: Building Your Inner Confidence 43
- Self-Compassion and Forgiveness 44
- Setting Boundaries for Self-Respect 46
- Nurturing Your Body and Mind 47
- Navigating the Ebbs and Flows of Self-Love 49
- Celebrating Your Self-Love Wins 51
- Case Study: Cultivating Self-Love in Action 52
- Exercise 1: Cultivating Self-Compassion Through Letter Writing 53
- Exercise 2: Nurturing Your Mind and Body Through Mindful Self-Care 55
- Self-Reflection Questions 56

CHAPTER 4: EMBRACING SELF-LOVE IN THE MODERN WORLD 59
- Too Busy for Self-Care? Squeezing Self-Care Into a Packed Schedule 59
- Digital Self-Love: Balancing Online Presence With Real Self-Worth 63
- Technological Tools for Self-Love 65
- Financial Self-Care in the Digital Economy 67
- Embracing Self-Love in the Modern World 71
- Practicing Radical Self-Acceptance in a Filtered World 73
- Nurturing Slow Living and Mindfulness in a Fast-Paced World 74
- Case Study: Navigating Self-Love in the Digital Age 75
- Exercise 1: Digital Detox Challenge 77
- Exercise 2: Aligning Your Online Presence With Your Authentic Self 79
- Self-Reflection Questions 80

CHAPTER 5: CULTIVATING A SELF-LOVE LIFESTYLE 83
- Living Authentically and Building Resilience 83
- Cultivating Joy and Fulfillment 86
- Self-Love in Relationships 88
- Finding Meaning and Purpose in Self-Love 91
- Self-Love as a Lifelong Practice 92
- Putting It All Together 94
- Case Study: Embracing a Self-Love Lifestyle 95
- Exercise 1: Crafting a Self-Love Manifesto 97
- Exercise 2: Cultivating Joy and Fulfillment Through a Self-Date 99
- Self-Reflection Questions 100

CONCLUSION 105

REFERENCES 108

SPECIAL BONUS!

Want this Bonus book for Free?

Get FREE, unlimited access to it and all my new books by joining the Fan Base!

Introduction

Life as a woman in this crazy world can be a wild ride. We're constantly being told how to look, how to act, and who to be by everyone from society to social media. It is enough to make your head spin and leave you feeling like you're never quite measuring up. But listen up, honey: You've got the power within you to break free from all that noise and start loving yourself exactly as you are, imperfections and all.

That is where *Self-Love Revolution* comes in, and let me tell you, this book is about to become your new best friend. It is like having a heart-to-heart with someone who's been through it all and is ready to spill the tea on how to cultivate genuine self-love and acceptance. No sugarcoating, no fluff, just real talk and practical advice to help you overcome whatever's holding you back from loving yourself fiercely.

As you dive into these pages, you'll get to the root of why we doubt ourselves and engage in that pesky negative self-talk. But don't worry, because *Self-Love Revolution* is coming in hot with targeted techniques to help you kick those bad habits to the curb. And let's not forget about the unique struggles that come with being a woman in the digital age—from the pressure to have the "perfect" body to the endless cycle of comparing ourselves to others on social media. This book isn't afraid to go there, and it has got real solutions and insights to help you navigate it all with strength and resilience.

But here's the thing: *Self-Love Revolution* isn't just a bunch of theories. It is packed with juicy real-life stories, hands-on exercises, and actionable steps you can take to put yourself first, set healthy boundaries, and create a life that truly lights you up inside. By the time you turn that last page, you'll be armed with the tools and the confidence to take on whatever life throws your way, all while loving yourself unapologetically.

So, whether you're a 20-something trying to find your way, a busy working mama juggling it all, or anyone in between who's ready to level up their self-love game, *Self-Love Revolution* is here for you. It is time to break up with self-doubt and start building the life you deserve—one filled with genuine joy, inner peace, and the kind of unshakable confidence that comes from truly having your own back.

If you're ready to join the self-love revolution, then grab this book, cozy up with a cup of tea, and let's get this party started. Your journey to a more fulfilling, joyful life begins now, and I can't wait to witness the magic that unfolds when you start loving yourself like you mean it.

In *Self-Love Revolution*, we'll dive deep into the many facets of self-love and explore how to cultivate it in every aspect of your life. You'll learn how to embrace your authentic self, celebrate your unique quirks and imperfections, and build unshakable self-esteem and confidence from the inside out. We'll talk about the importance of setting boundaries, practicing self-compassion, and surrounding yourself with people who lift you up and support your journey.

But we won't stop there. This book also tackles the tough stuff, like overcoming perfectionism, silencing your inner critic, and healing from past wounds and traumas. You'll discover powerful techniques for reframing negative self-talk, letting go of limiting beliefs, and cultivating a growth mindset that allows you to learn and evolve through life's challenges.

And because we know that self-love isn't just an inside job, *Self-Love Revolution* also explores how to navigate the modern world with grace and resilience. From practicing self-care in a busy, fast-paced world to building authentic relationships and finding your purpose, this book has you covered. You'll learn how to use technology and social media in a way that uplifts and inspires you rather than dragging you down and how to cultivate a sense of meaning and fulfillment that goes beyond external validation and approval.

Throughout the book, you'll find practical exercises, prompts, and tools to help you put these lessons into action and make self-love a daily practice. Whether it is through journaling, meditation, or creative self-expression, you'll discover the practices that work best for you and your unique journey.

But perhaps most importantly, *Self-Love Revolution* is a reminder that you are not alone. By sharing my own story and the stories of countless other women who have transformed their lives through radical self-love, I hope to create a sense of community and connection that empowers you to keep going, even on the tough days. Because here's the truth: When we come together and support each other in our journeys of self-love and growth, we create a ripple effect of healing and transformation that touches every corner of our lives and the world around us.

So, if you're ready to say goodbye to self-doubt, self-criticism, and self-sabotage and hello to a life of unapologetic self-love and unstoppable confidence, welcome to the *Self-Love Revolution*. Let's dive in and start creating the life you've always dreamed of—one fierce act of self-love at a time.

Chapter 1:

Understanding Self-Love

Let's dive a little deeper into this whole self-love thing, shall we? I know it can feel like a daunting concept, especially if you're someone who's been taught to put everyone else's needs before your own. But trust me, learning to love yourself is one of the most important things you can do—not just for your own well-being but for the well-being of those around you.

The Basics of Self-Love

Let's start with the basics. Self-love is about treating yourself with the same kindness, compassion, and respect that you would show to someone you care about deeply. It is about accepting yourself, flaws and all, and recognizing that your worth isn't contingent on your accomplishments, appearance, or relationship status.

I know, easier said than done, right? We live in a society that is constantly telling us we need to be thinner, prettier, smarter, more successful—the list goes on and on. It is no wonder so many of us struggle with self-doubt and insecurity. But here's the thing: Buying into those messages is a surefire way to make yourself miserable.

Breaking Free From Negative Messages

So, how do you break free from that cycle? It starts with recognizing that those messages are BS. They're designed to make you feel like you're not enough, so you'll buy more products or conform to someone else's idea of who you should be. But the truth is, you are enough, just as you are.

I know some of you might be thinking, *But I have so many flaws and imperfections—how can I possibly love myself?* And I get it. We all have things we wish we could change about ourselves. But here's the thing: Those flaws and imperfections are what make you unique. They're what make you human. And when you learn to embrace them, rather than trying to hide or change them, you open yourself up to a whole new level of self-acceptance and self-love.

Seeking Support on Your Self-Love Journey

Let's be real: Loving yourself isn't always easy, especially if you've experienced trauma or hardship in your life. It can be hard to let go of the negative beliefs and patterns that have been ingrained in you over time. That is why it is so important to seek out support and resources when you need them.

That might mean talking to a therapist or counselor who can help you work through your past experiences and develop healthier coping mechanisms. It might mean joining a support group or finding a community of like-minded people who are on a similar journey. Or, it might mean educating yourself about self-love and self-care through books, podcasts, or online resources.

The important thing is to remember that you don't have to go it alone. There are people and resources out there who can help you on your self-love journey, and it is okay to ask for help when you need it.

Celebrating Your Strengths and Successes

Self-love isn't just about working through your past traumas and challenges. It is also about celebrating your strengths and successes and treating yourself with the same enthusiasm and joy that you would a close friend.

Think about it: When your best friend accomplishes something amazing, do you downplay it or brush it off? Of course not! You celebrate with them, tell them how proud you are of them, and encourage them to keep going. So, why not do the same for yourself?

When you have a win, no matter how small, take a moment to acknowledge it and give yourself a pat on the back. When you do something kind for yourself, like taking a relaxing bath or going for a walk in nature, savor the experience and let yourself feel the joy and peace that comes with it.

And when you have a setback or make a mistake, don't beat yourself up about it. Instead, treat yourself with the same compassion and understanding that you would a friend going through a tough time. Remind yourself that everyone makes mistakes and that it is okay to be imperfect.

Self-Love Isn't Selfish

Now, I know some of you might be thinking, *But isn't all this self-love stuff a bit selfish? Shouldn't I be focusing on others instead of myself?* And I get where you're coming from. We're often taught that putting others' needs before our own is the right thing to do.

But here's the thing: You can't pour from an empty cup. If you're constantly giving and giving without taking time to recharge and take care of yourself, you're going to burn out. And when you're burnt out, you're no good to anyone—not your family, not your friends, not your community.

Self-love isn't selfish. It is necessary. It is what allows you to show up as your best self in all areas of your life. When you love and care for yourself, you have more energy, more patience, and more compassion to give to others.

Incorporating Self-Love Into Your Daily Life

How do you start incorporating more self-love into your life? It can be as simple as taking a few minutes each day to do something that brings you joy, whether that is reading a book, listening to music, or taking a bubble bath. It can be setting boundaries with people who drain your energy or saying no to commitments that don't align with your values.

It can be practicing self-compassion when you're feeling down and reminding yourself that you're doing your best. It can be surrounding yourself with people who lift you up and support you rather than tear you down.

It can also be making a conscious effort to change how you talk to yourself. Instead of focusing on your flaws and shortcomings, try to reframe your thoughts in a more positive light. Instead of saying, "I'm so stupid for making that mistake," try saying, "I'm human, and it is okay to make mistakes. I'll learn from this and do better next time."

It might feel awkward or uncomfortable at first, but the more you practice self-love, the more natural it will become. As you start to see the benefits in your own life—more confidence, resilience, and joy—you'll wonder why you didn't start sooner.

The Lifelong Practice of Self-Love

Here's the thing: Self-love isn't a one-and-done kind of deal. It is a lifelong practice, and there will be ups and downs along the way. There will be days when you feel like you're on top of the world and days when you feel like you're struggling to keep your head above water.

And that is okay. It is all part of the journey. The important thing is to keep showing up for yourself, even on the tough days, and to keep reminding yourself of your worth and your value, even when the world tries to tell you otherwise.

Because at the end of the day, you are the only person who will be with you for your entire life. You are the only person who can truly love and accept yourself, flaws and all. When you learn to do that, everything else falls into place.

Your Self-Love Challenge

My challenge to you is this: Start small. Start with one thing you can do today to show yourself a little extra love and kindness—and then keep going. Keep building on that foundation, day by day, until self-love becomes as natural to you as breathing.

When you have those moments of doubt or insecurity, when you feel like you're not enough or you're too much, remember this: You are worthy of love and acceptance, just as you are. You are enough, exactly as you are. You have the power to create a life that feels authentic, fulfilling, and joyful.

So, go out there and love yourself like your life depends on it. Because, in a way, it does. When you learn to love and accept yourself fully, you open yourself up to a world of possibilities and opportunities. You become unstoppable.

The Ripple Effect of Self-Love

Who knows? Maybe one day, you'll be the one inspiring someone else to start their own self-love journey. Maybe you'll be the one reminding them of their worth and value, even when the world tries to tell them otherwise.

Because that is the thing about self-love: It is contagious. When you start to radiate self-acceptance and self-compassion, it has a ripple effect on everyone around you. You become a beacon of hope and inspiration for others who are struggling to love themselves.

So, let's make a pact. Let's commit to showing up for ourselves, even when it is hard. Let's challenge the messages that tell us we're not enough and replace them with a narrative of self-love and self-acceptance. Let's support each other on this journey and celebrate each other's successes along the way.

Because at the end of the day, we're all in this together. We're all worthy of love and acceptance, just as we are. And when we learn to love ourselves fully and unapologetically, we create a world where everyone can thrive.

The Most Important Job You'll Ever Have

Go forth and love yourself like it is your job. Because, in a way, it is. It is the most important job you'll ever have. I promise you, it is worth every ounce of effort you put into it.

But don't just take my word for it. Start experimenting with self-love in your own life and see what happens. Notice how your relationship with yourself starts to shift. Notice how you become more resilient, more confident, and more at peace.

If you ever need a reminder of why self-love is so important, just think about the people in your life who you love and admire most. Chances are, they're the ones who radiate self-acceptance and self-compassion. They're the ones who inspire you to be your best self simply by being theirs.

That is the power of self-love. It is not just about feeling good in the moment; it is about creating a life that feels authentic, fulfilling, and joyful. It is about showing up as your best self in all areas of your life and inspiring others to do the same.

The best part? It all starts with you. You have the power to start your self-love journey today and to keep showing up for yourself, day after day, year after year.

What are you waiting for? Start small, and start now. Your future self will thank you.

Overcoming Obstacles on Your Self-Love Journey

I know that embarking on a self-love journey can feel overwhelming at times. There will be obstacles along the way—negative self-talk, past traumas, societal pressures, you name it. But here's the thing: Those obstacles don't define you. They don't have to hold you back from loving yourself fully and completely.

When you encounter an obstacle on your self-love journey, the first step is acknowledging it. Don't try to push it away or pretend it doesn't exist. Instead, take a deep breath and say to yourself, "Okay, this is hard. This is uncomfortable. But I can handle it."

Then, get curious about the obstacle. What is it trying to teach you? What fears or beliefs is it bringing up for you? What do you need to move through it?

Sometimes, the answer might be as simple as taking a break and practicing some extra self-care. Other times, it might mean seeking additional support, whether that is from a therapist, a trusted friend, or a self-help book.

No matter what, remember this: You are stronger than your obstacles. You have the resilience and the wisdom to overcome anything that comes your way. When you do, you'll emerge even stronger and more in love with yourself than before.

The Beauty of Imperfection

One of the biggest obstacles to self-love is the belief that we have to be perfect to be worthy of love and acceptance. We put so much pressure on ourselves to have the perfect body, the perfect career, the perfect relationship—and when we inevitably fall short, we beat ourselves up and tell ourselves we're not good enough.

But here's the thing: Perfection is a myth. It is an unattainable standard that keeps us stuck in a cycle of self-doubt and self-criticism. The truth is that our imperfections are what make us beautiful. They're what make us human.

When you start to embrace your imperfections, you open yourself up to a whole new level of self-love and self-acceptance. You stop trying to hide your flaws and start celebrating them as part of what makes you unique and special.

The next time you catch yourself striving for perfection, take a step back and remind yourself that you are enough, just as you are. Embrace your quirks, your mistakes, your imperfections—and watch as your self-love grows deeper and more profound.

The Gift of Self-Love

At the end of the day, self-love is a gift. It is a gift that only you can give yourself, and it is a gift that keeps on giving. When you love yourself fully and completely, you show up in the world as a brighter, more authentic version of yourself. You inspire others to do the same simply by being you.

And here's the best part: Self-love is available to you right here, right now. You don't have to wait until you've lost the weight, got the promotion, or found the perfect partner. You can start loving yourself today, exactly as you are.

Take a deep breath, put your hand on your heart, and repeat after me: "I am worthy of love and acceptance, just as I am. I choose to love and accept myself, fully and completely, today and every day." Then, go out there and live your life from a place of deep, unshakable self-love. Watch as your world transforms before your very eyes. Watch as you become the person you were always meant to be.

Because that is the power of self-love; it is the power to change your life and the world around you, one moment at a time, and it all starts with you.

Case Study: Sarah's Self-Love Journey

Sarah was a successful lawyer in her mid-30s who seemed to have it all together on the outside—a thriving career, a beautiful home, and a busy social life. But inside, Sarah struggled with deep-seated feelings of inadequacy and self-doubt. She constantly compared herself to others and felt like she was never good enough, no matter how much she achieved.

One day, after a particularly stressful week at work, Sarah hit a breaking point. She realized that her lack of self-love was impacting every area of her life—her relationships, her work performance, and her overall happiness. She decided it was time to make a change.

Sarah started small by setting aside just 10 minutes each morning for self-care. She used this time to journal, meditate, or do a quick yoga sequence—whatever made her feel calm and centered. She also started paying attention to her self-talk and made a conscious effort to replace negative thoughts with more compassionate ones.

As Sarah continued to prioritize self-love, she began to notice shifts in her life. She felt more confident at work and started speaking up more in meetings. She set better boundaries in her relationships and learned to say no to commitments that didn't serve her. Perhaps most importantly, she started feeling a sense of inner peace and contentment that she had never experienced before.

Sarah's self-love journey wasn't always easy. There were days when she struggled with old patterns of self-doubt and criticism, but she committed to showing up for herself each day, even in small ways. Over time, self-love became a non-negotiable part of her daily routine, and she saw the ripple effects in every area of her life.

Through her experience, Sarah learned that self-love isn't selfish or indulgent; it is a necessity for a happy, fulfilling life. She now shares her story with others and encourages them to start their own self-love journeys, one small step at a time.

Cultivating a Growth Mindset

As you start on your self-love journey, embracing a growth mindset is one of the most powerful shifts you can make. This means viewing challenges and setbacks not as failures or indictments of your worth but as opportunities for learning, growth, and self-discovery.

When we approach life with a fixed mindset, we believe our abilities, traits, and potential are predetermined and unchangeable. We fear making mistakes or facing obstacles because we see them as reflections of our inherent inadequacy or lack of talent. This can lead to a vicious cycle of self-doubt, avoidance, and stagnation, where we hold ourselves back from pursuing our dreams and showing up fully in the world.

In contrast, a growth mindset is founded on the belief that we can always learn, evolve, and expand our capabilities. When we encounter roadblocks or fall short of our goals, we view these experiences as valuable feedback and fuel for our ongoing development. We embrace challenges as chances to stretch ourselves and discover new strengths and skills.

Cultivating a growth mindset is essential for self-love because it allows us to extend compassion and patience to ourselves as we navigate the ups and downs of personal growth. Instead of beating ourselves up for not being perfect or having it all figured out, we can celebrate our progress, no matter how small or incremental. We can reframe our inner dialogue from one of self-judgment to one of self-encouragement, cheering ourselves on as we take brave steps outside our comfort zone.

To start cultivating a growth mindset, try reframing your perception of failure and setbacks. When you encounter a disappointment or roadblock, ask yourself: "What can I learn from this experience? How can I use this as an opportunity to grow and become a better version of myself?"

Another powerful practice is celebrating your efforts and progress, not just your achievements. Acknowledge yourself for showing up, taking risks, and putting in the hard work—even if the outcome isn't what you hoped for. Remember, the journey of growth is just as important as the destination.

Finally, surround yourself with people and resources that support and inspire a growth mindset. Seek out mentors, friends, and communities that celebrate learning, experimentation, and personal development. Read books, listen to podcasts, and engage with content that expands your mind and challenges you to think in new ways.

By embracing a growth mindset, you open yourself up to a world of possibility and potential. You become more resilient in the face of setbacks, more adaptable to change, and more confident in your ability to create the life you desire. Most importantly, you deepen your capacity for self-love and self-acceptance, knowing that you are always worthy of growth, learning, and becoming your best self.

Finding Your Self-Love Tribe

One of the most powerful ways to support your self-love journey is to surround yourself with people who uplift, inspire, and accept you for who you truly are. While the work of self-love is ultimately an inside job, having a supportive community can make all the difference in staying committed to your path and weathering the inevitable ups and downs.

Unfortunately, not everyone in our lives may be equipped to support us in the way we need. Some people may be stuck in their own patterns of self-doubt or self-criticism and unconsciously project those beliefs onto us. Others may feel threatened or uncomfortable with the changes we're making and try to discourage us from rocking the boat.

That is why it is so important to be intentional about cultivating a self-love tribe—a group of people who share your values, celebrate your growth, and have your back no matter what. These are the people who will cheer you on when you're feeling low, challenge you to stay true to yourself, and remind you of your inherent worthiness and potential.

So, how do you go about finding your self-love tribe? Start by getting clarity on the qualities and values that are most important to you in your relationships. What kind of energy and support do you need to thrive? What shared interests or passions do you want to explore with others?

Once you have a sense of what you're looking for, start putting yourself out there and connecting with like-minded individuals. This might mean joining a support group or online community related to self-love or personal growth. It could involve attending workshops, retreats, or events that align with your values and interests. Or, it might simply mean reaching out to friends or acquaintances who inspire you and inviting them to connect more deeply.

As you begin to build your self-love tribe, be mindful of the energy and dynamics in your interactions. Pay attention to how you feel before, during, and after spending time with each person. Do you feel uplifted, inspired, and accepted? Or, do you feel drained, judged, or deflated?

Remember, your self-love tribe should be a source of nourishment and support, not stress or depletion. Be willing to set boundaries and protect your energy as needed, even if it means letting go of relationships that no longer serve you.

At the same time, be open to the vulnerability and intimacy that comes with true connection. Allow yourself to be seen and heard in your authentic truth, and extend the same compassion and acceptance to others. Celebrate each other's successes, hold space for each other's struggles, and remind each other of the beauty and strength that lies within.

Building a self-love tribe takes time, effort, and discernment. But the rewards are immeasurable, not only for your own journey but for the collective healing and transformation of the world. By coming together in shared purpose and love, we create a powerful ripple effect of positive change that touches every corner of our lives and communities.

So, don't be afraid to reach out, connect, and lean on your self-love tribe. Together, we rise higher, shine brighter, and create a world where every person knows their inherent worthiness and belongs to a community of love and support.

Exercise 1: Self-Love Affirmation Practice

1. Take out a piece of paper and a pen. At the top of the page, write, "I am worthy of love and acceptance, just as I am."

2. Below that statement, write down 3–5 affirmations that resonate with you. These could be statements like "I trust my intuition and make choices that align with my values," "I am capable of overcoming any challenge that comes my way," or "I radiate love and compassion to myself and others."

3. Take a few deep breaths and sit in a comfortable position. Close your eyes and begin repeating your affirmations to yourself, either out loud or silently in your mind.

4. As you repeat each affirmation, really try to feel the truth of the words in your body. Imagine yourself embodying the qualities you are affirming.

5. Continue repeating your affirmations for at least five minutes, or longer if you wish. Notice how you feel before, during, and after the practice.

6. Repeat this exercise daily for at least a week and observe any shifts in your mindset and self-talk. You can use the same affirmations each day or come up with new ones as you feel called to.

The goal of this exercise is to train your mind to focus on positive, self-loving thoughts until they become habitual and automatic. Over time, this practice can help to reprogram negative self-talk and boost self-esteem and confidence.

Exercise 2: Mirror Work

1. Find a quiet, private space where you can be alone with a mirror. Make sure you have at least 5–10 minutes of uninterrupted time.

2. Stand or sit in front of the mirror and take a few deep breaths to center yourself. Look into your own eyes and notice any sensations or emotions that arise.

3. Begin speaking to yourself in the mirror as if you were talking to a dear friend. Use a kind, compassionate tone and avoid any self-criticism or judgment.

4. Start by acknowledging any challenges or struggles you are currently facing. You might say something like, "I see that you are feeling overwhelmed with work right now, and that is completely valid and understandable."

5. Then, offer yourself some words of encouragement and support. You might say something like, "I want you to know that you are doing your best, and that is enough. You are strong, capable, and resilient, even when things feel tough."

6. Continue speaking to yourself in this way for at least 5–10 minutes. Focus on highlighting your positive qualities and strengths, and offer compassion for any perceived flaws or mistakes.

7. When you feel complete, take a few deep breaths and thank yourself for showing up for this practice. Notice how you feel in your mind and body.

8. Repeat this exercise regularly, ideally at least once per week, to cultivate a practice of self-love and self-acceptance.

The goal of mirror work is to develop a loving, compassionate relationship with yourself. By speaking to yourself with kindness and understanding, you can begin to shift your inner dialogue and build a foundation of self-love and self-respect.

Remember, self-love is a lifelong practice, and there is no finish line. Be patient and compassionate with yourself as you navigate the ups and downs of your journey. Trust that every small step you take toward loving yourself more fully is valuable and worthwhile.

Self-Reflection Questions

As you've read through this chapter on understanding and cultivating self-love, you may have found yourself nodding along in recognition or feeling a spark of inspiration to begin your own self-love journey. The concepts and practices outlined here are a powerful starting point, but the real magic happens when you apply them to your own unique life and experiences. To support you in integrating these teachings and taking your self-love practice to the next level, I invite you to reflect on the following questions. Find a quiet space, grab a journal or a trusted friend, and allow yourself to explore your answers with openness, curiosity, and compassion. Remember, this is a judgment-free zone. There are no right or wrong ways to approach your self-love journey, only the way that feels most authentic and nourishing to you.

1. What are some of the negative messages or beliefs about yourself that you have internalized over time? How have these messages impacted your self-esteem and sense of self-worth?

2. Reflect on a time when you showed yourself compassion and understanding, even in the face of a mistake or failure. How did it feel to extend kindness to yourself in that moment? What shifted in your mindset or emotions as a result?

3. Consider the people in your life who you admire and respect. What qualities do they embody that you would like to

cultivate more of in yourself? How can you start practicing those qualities in your own life, even in small ways?

4. What are some of the ways you typically speak to yourself, especially in moments of stress, anxiety, or self-doubt? If you were to speak to a loved one in the same situation, how might your language and tone shift to be more supportive and encouraging?

5. Identify one area of your life where you tend to be the hardest on yourself, whether it is your appearance, work performance, relationships, etc. What would it look like to approach this area with more self-love and self-acceptance? What small steps can you take to start shifting your mindset and habits?

6. Reflect on a time when you put someone else's needs before your own, even when it left you feeling drained or resentful. How can you start setting better boundaries and prioritizing your own self-care, even in the face of external pressures or expectations?

7. What activities, practices, or experiences make you feel most alive, joyful, and connected to yourself? How can you start incorporating more of these moments of authentic self-expression and self-love into your daily life?

8. Imagine yourself five years from now, living a life filled with deep self-love, self-acceptance, and self-compassion. What would be different about your relationships, work, habits, and overall sense of well-being? What steps can you start taking today to move closer to that vision?

Remember, there are no right or wrong answers to these questions. The goal is simply to create space for honest self-reflection and to start building greater awareness around your self-love journey. Trust whatever insights and emotions arise for you, and be gentle with yourself as you explore this transformative practice.

SPECIAL BONUS!

Want this Bonus book for Free?

Get FREE, unlimited access to it and all my new books by joining the Fan Base!

Chapter 2:

Overcoming Barriers to Self-Love

So, you've decided to embark on this wild and wonderful journey of self-love. That is fantastic! Give yourself a pat on the back because taking that first step is often the hardest part.

But here's the thing: The road to self-love is not always a smooth one. Along the way, you're going to encounter some obstacles—roadblocks that try to keep you stuck in old patterns of self-doubt, self-criticism, and self-sabotage.

These barriers to self-love can take many forms. Maybe it is that little voice in your head that is always telling you you're not good enough. Maybe it is the perfectionism that keeps you stuck in a cycle of procrastination and self-doubt. Maybe it is the toxic relationships that drain your energy and make you feel small.

Whatever your barriers to self-love may be, know this: They are not insurmountable. With a little bit of awareness, a lot of self-compassion, and a willingness to do the work, you can break through these barriers and cultivate a deep, lasting love for yourself.

In this chapter, we're going to dive into seven of the most common barriers to self-love: negative self-talk, perfectionism, toxic relationships, fear of judgment, self-doubt, past mistakes, and fear of failure. We'll explore why these barriers are so sneaky and persistent and how they can keep us stuck in patterns of self-sabotage and self-loathing.

More importantly, we'll talk about how to overcome these barriers. We'll discuss practical strategies for letting go of negative self-talk, embracing imperfection, setting boundaries in relationships, and cultivating self-compassion and self-forgiveness. We'll explore how to reframe failure as a learning opportunity and how to build resilience in the face of setbacks and challenges.

Throughout this chapter, I encourage you to approach these barriers with curiosity and compassion. Remember that they are not a reflection of your worth or value as a person; they are simply patterns and beliefs you've picked up along the way, often without even realizing it.

As you work to break through these barriers, be patient with yourself. Self-love is not a destination—it is a journey full of ups and downs and twists and turns. There will be days when you feel like you're making progress and days when you feel like you're taking two steps back.

No matter what, keep going. Keep showing up for yourself, even on the hard days. Keep practicing self-compassion and self-forgiveness, even when it feels impossible. And most importantly, keep believing in your inherent worth and value, no matter what your barriers try to tell you.

Because at the end of the day, you deserve to love yourself fully and completely. You deserve to feel confident, empowered, and at peace with who you are. With a little bit of work and a lot of self-love, you can get there—one small step at a time.

So, let's dive in, shall we? Let's explore these barriers to self-love and learn how to break through them once and for all. Because on the other side of these barriers lies a life of joy, fulfillment, and deep, unshakable self-love—and that, my friends, is worth fighting for.

Letting Go of Negative Self-Talk

First up, let's talk about that pesky little voice in your head. You know the one—it is always telling you that you're not good enough, smart enough, pretty enough, whatever enough. I'm here to tell you that that voice is a liar, and the more you listen to it, the more power it has over you.

So, how do you shut up that voice? It starts with mindfulness. Pay attention to the thoughts that run through your head, and when you catch yourself engaging in negative self-talk, stop and reframe it. Instead of saying, "I'm so stupid," try saying, "I made a mistake, but

I'm learning and growing." Instead of saying, "I'm not good enough," try saying, "I am worthy and deserving of love and respect."

It might feel weird at first, but the more you practice replacing those negative thoughts with positive affirmations, the easier it will become. Before you know it, that little voice in your head will start to sound a whole lot kinder.

Letting Go of Perfectionism

Next up, let's talk about perfectionism. Oh, perfectionism. It is like the overachieving cousin of negative self-talk. It tells you that anything less than perfect is unacceptable and that if you can't do something perfectly, you shouldn't do it at all.

But here's the thing: Perfectionism is a myth. It is an unattainable standard that keeps us stuck in a cycle of self-doubt and self-criticism. When we inevitably fall short of that standard, we beat ourselves up and tell ourselves we're not good enough.

So, how do you break free from the perfection trap? It starts with embracing imperfection. Celebrate your progress, no matter how small. Focus on the journey, not just the destination. Most importantly, remember that your worth is not tied to your achievements or your ability to meet some arbitrary standard of perfection.

Releasing Toxic Relationships

Now, let's talk about the people in your life. Specifically, the ones who drain your energy, lower your self-esteem, and hold you back from being your best self. Those, my friends, are toxic relationships. If you want to truly love yourself, you need to let them go.

I know, easier said than done, right? But you deserve to be surrounded by people who lift you up, not tear you down—people who support your dreams and celebrate your successes, people who love you for who you are, not who they think you should be.

So, how do you release toxic relationships? It starts with recognizing them for what they are. Pay attention to how you feel when you're around certain people. Do they make you feel drained, anxious, or insecure? Do they constantly criticize you or put you down? If so, it might be time to distance yourself.

Now, I'm not saying you have to cut these people out of your life completely (although, in some cases, that might be necessary). You can start by setting boundaries. Let them know what behavior is and isn't acceptable. If they continue to cross those boundaries, it might be time to re-evaluate the relationship.

As you release those toxic relationships, make sure to actively cultivate positive ones. Surround yourself with people who inspire, support, and bring out the best in you. Trust me, it makes all the difference.

Overcoming the Fear of Judgment

Okay, let's talk about the elephant in the room: the fear of judgment—the fear of not being liked, of being criticized, of being rejected. It is a biggie, and it can keep us stuck in a cycle of people-pleasing and self-doubt.

Remember that you will never be able to please everyone, and trying to do so will only leave you feeling exhausted and inauthentic. How do you overcome the fear of judgment? It starts with strengthening your internal validation.

What does that mean? It means learning to love and accept yourself, regardless of what others think. It means affirming your own worth and value, even in the face of criticism or rejection. It means being true to yourself, even if that means ruffling a few feathers along the way.

I'm not saying it is easy. We're social creatures, and the desire to be liked and accepted is deeply ingrained in us. However, the more you practice self-love and self-acceptance, the less you'll need external validation to feel good about yourself.

Start by setting small goals for yourself. Maybe it is wearing that outfit you love, even if it is not "in style." Maybe it is speaking up in a meeting, even if you're afraid of sounding stupid. Maybe it is saying no to a request that doesn't align with your values, even if you're worried about disappointing someone.

Each time you do one of these things, take a moment to celebrate your bravery and authenticity. Remind yourself that you are worthy and deserving of love and respect, no matter what anyone else thinks.

Letting Go of Self-Doubt

Now, let's talk about self-doubt—that nagging feeling that you're not good enough, smart enough, or talented enough to achieve your goals and dreams. It can be paralyzing, keeping us stuck in a cycle of inaction and fear.

But self-doubt is a liar. It is a false belief that keeps us playing small and holding ourselves back from our full potential. The more we listen to it, the more power it has over us.

So, how do you let go of self-doubt? It starts with taking action, even in the face of fear. Set small, achievable goals for yourself, and celebrate each accomplishment along the way. Focus on progress, not perfection, and remind yourself that you are capable and deserving of success, no matter what your self-doubt tries to tell you.

Here's a little secret: Everyone experiences self-doubt at some point. Even the most successful, confident people have moments of insecurity and fear. The difference is they don't let it stop them. They feel the fear and do it anyway.

The next time self-doubt creeps in, take a deep breath and remind yourself of all the times you've overcome challenges and achieved your goals. Remind yourself of your strengths, talents, and unique gifts. Then, take that first step, no matter how small or scary it may feel.

Healing From Past Mistakes

We've all made mistakes. We've all done things we're not proud of, said things we wish we could take back, and made choices we regret. If we're not careful, those mistakes can haunt us, keeping us stuck in a cycle of guilt and shame.

But here's the thing: Your mistakes do not define you. They are not a reflection of your worth or your value as a person. They are simply learning opportunities, chances to grow and evolve and become the best version of yourself.

So, how do you heal from past mistakes? It starts with forgiveness. Forgiveness of others, yes, but most importantly, forgiveness of yourself. Acknowledge the mistake, learn from it, and then let it go. Choose to move forward rather than dwelling on the past.

I know that is easier said than done. Forgiveness is a process that takes time and practice. Each time you choose to forgive yourself, you open up a little more space for self-love and self-acceptance.

And here's the beautiful thing: When you learn to forgive yourself, you also learn to extend that forgiveness to others. You become more compassionate and understanding and able to see the humanity in everyone around you.

The next time you find yourself dwelling on a past mistake, take a deep breath and remind yourself that you are not defined by your errors. Remind yourself that you are worthy of forgiveness and love, no matter what. Then, take a step forward, armed with the knowledge that you are growing and evolving every single day.

Letting Go of the Fear of Failure

Last but not least, let's talk about the big one: the fear of failure—the fear that keeps us stuck in our comfort zones, afraid to take risks or try new things, the fear that tells us it is better to play it safe than to risk falling flat on our faces.

But failure is not the enemy. In fact, it is a necessary part of growth and success. Every successful person has failed at some point—often many times—on their way to achieving their goals. The difference is they didn't let those failures define them or hold them back.

So, how do you let go of the fear of failure? It starts with reframing failure as a learning opportunity. Instead of seeing it as a reflection of your worth or ability, see it as a chance to learn, grow, and become better.

And here's a little secret: The more you embrace failure, the less scary it becomes. When you know that failure is not the end of the world—that it is simply a stepping stone on the path to success—you become more willing to take risks and try new things.

The next time you find yourself holding back because of the fear of failure, take a deep breath and remind yourself that failure is not fatal. Remind yourself of all the times you've bounced back from setbacks and challenges and all the lessons you've learned along the way. Then, take that leap, knowing that no matter what happens, you will come out the other side stronger and wiser than before.

Cultivating Self-Trust and Inner Wisdom

As you navigate the journey of self-love, one of the most powerful tools you have at your disposal is your inner wisdom and intuition. Learning to trust yourself and your instincts is a crucial part of breaking free from the barriers that hold you back from loving yourself fully.

However, it can be challenging to tune into our inner voice in a world that constantly bombards us with external messages and expectations. We may have learned to doubt ourselves, second-guess our decisions, or seek validation and approval from others rather than trusting our judgment.

Cultivating self-trust means learning to listen to and honor your thoughts, feelings, and desires, even when they go against the grain of what others expect or demand of you. It means developing a deep sense of confidence in your ability to make choices that align with your values, goals, and well-being.

One way to start building self-trust is to practice making small, low-stakes decisions without seeking input or approval from others. This might mean choosing what to wear, what to eat, or how to spend your free time based solely on your own preferences and instincts. As you begin to trust yourself in these small ways, you can gradually build up to making bigger, more significant decisions with greater ease and confidence.

Another key aspect of cultivating self-trust is learning to differentiate between your inner wisdom and the limiting beliefs or fears that may be masquerading as intuition. Sometimes, what we perceive as our gut instinct may actually be a manifestation of our self-doubt, insecurity, or past traumas.

To help discern between true inner wisdom and false fears, try checking in with your body and emotions when making decisions or facing challenges. Notice any physical sensations, such as tightness, tension, or a sinking feeling in your stomach that may indicate that something is off or not aligned with your authentic self. On the other hand, pay attention to feelings of expansiveness, excitement, or a deep sense of rightness that may signal that you are on the right track.

It can also be helpful to practice self-reflection and journaling as a way to gain clarity and insight into your inner landscape. By taking time to explore your thoughts, beliefs, and patterns, you can start to identify and challenge any limiting narratives that may be holding you back from trusting yourself fully.

Ultimately, cultivating self-trust is about developing a deep and unshakeable relationship with yourself. It is about learning to honor your needs, desires, and boundaries, even in the face of external pressure or disapproval. It is about believing in your inherent wisdom, resilience, and worthiness, no matter what obstacles or challenges you may face along the way.

By committing to the practice of self-trust, you open yourself up to a whole new level of self-love, self-respect, and personal empowerment. You become the ultimate authority in your own life, guided by your inner compass and fueled by the unshakeable belief in your ability to create a life that feels authentic, fulfilling, and true to who you are.

Embracing Vulnerability and Authentic Connection

One of the biggest barriers to self-love is the fear of vulnerability—the fear of being seen, heard, and accepted for who we truly are, flaws and all. In a culture that often prizes perfection, achievement, and self-sufficiency, it can feel risky or even shameful to reveal our true selves and risk rejection or judgment from others.

However, the truth is that vulnerability is not a weakness but a profound strength and a necessary ingredient for deep, authentic connection and self-love. When we have the courage to show up as our true selves, we create space for genuine intimacy, empathy, and understanding—both with ourselves and others.

Brené Brown, a renowned researcher and author on vulnerability and shame, defines vulnerability as "uncertainty, risk, and emotional exposure." It is the willingness to be seen and heard, even when there's no guarantee of a positive outcome. It is the courage to share our stories, struggles, and true selves, even when it feels scary or uncomfortable.

Embracing vulnerability in the context of self-love means learning to accept and even celebrate all parts of yourself—not only the shiny, successful, or socially acceptable parts but also the messy, imperfect, and deeply human parts. It means giving yourself permission to be a work in progress, to make mistakes, and to be honest about your struggles and challenges.

One way to start practicing vulnerability is to share something authentic and true about yourself with a trusted friend, family member, or therapist. This might mean opening up about a past experience you've been holding onto with shame or secrecy or revealing a dream or desire that feels risky or uncertain. As you begin to share more of your authentic self with others, notice how it feels to be seen and accepted for who you truly are.

Another way to cultivate vulnerability is through creative self-expression, such as writing, art, music, or dance. By allowing yourself to express your emotions, experiences, and inner world in a raw and unfiltered way, you create a powerful outlet for vulnerability and self-discovery.

It is important to note that embracing vulnerability does not mean oversharing or disregarding your own boundaries and safety. It is about discernment—choosing when, where, and with whom to be vulnerable based on a foundation of self-trust and self-respect.

Ultimately, embracing vulnerability is about reclaiming the parts of yourself that you've been hiding or suppressing out of fear or shame. It is about learning to love and accept yourself fully, even in the face of uncertainty or discomfort. It is about creating deeper, more authentic connections with others based on shared humanity, empathy, and understanding.

As you practice vulnerability in the context of self-love, you may find that it becomes easier and more natural over time. You may start to feel a greater sense of freedom, authenticity, and self-acceptance, as well as a deeper sense of connection and belonging with others who share your values and experiences.

Remember, vulnerability is not about being perfect or having it all figured out; it is about being willing to show up as your true self, with all your beautiful imperfections and complexities. By embracing vulnerability, you open yourself up to a whole new level of self-love, self-discovery, and authentic connection—both with yourself and the world around you.

Embracing the Journey

That was a lot, wasn't it? Remember: Overcoming these barriers to self-love is not a one-time event. It is a lifelong journey, full of ups and downs and twists and turns—and that is okay.

The beauty of self-love is that it is not about perfection. It is not about having it all figured out, never making mistakes, or always feeling confident and self-assured. It is about showing up for yourself, day after day, no matter what life throws your way.

It is about learning to be kind to yourself, even on your worst days. It is about celebrating your strengths and embracing your imperfections. It is about surrounding yourself with people who lift you up and inspire you to be your best self.

Most importantly, it is about believing in yourself—believing that you are worthy of love, respect, and success, no matter what anyone else says or thinks, believing that you have the power to create the life you want, one small step at a time.

As you continue on this journey of self-love, remember to be patient with yourself. Remember to celebrate your progress, no matter how small. Remember that you are not alone—that there is a whole community of people out there cheering you on and supporting you every step of the way.

Because at the end of the day, self-love is not a destination. It is a practice—a daily choice to show up for yourself, to be kind to yourself, to believe in yourself. The more you practice, the easier it becomes.

So, keep going, my friends. Keep showing up for yourself, even on the hard days. Keep letting go of the things that hold you back and embracing the things that lift you up. Keep believing in your own worth and value, no matter what.

Keep loving yourself—fiercely, unapologetically, and with every ounce of your being. Because you, my dear, are worth it. You are worth every bit of love and respect and success that this world has to offer—and don't you ever forget it.

Case Study: Overcoming Perfectionism and Embracing Authenticity

Jasmine was a high-achieving college student who had always prided herself on her academic success and flawless appearance. But beneath her polished exterior, Jasmine struggled with intense perfectionism and a fear of judgment from others. She spent hours studying for exams, obsessing over every detail of her assignments, and curating her social media presence to project an image of effortless perfection.

Despite her many accomplishments, Jasmine never felt good enough. She constantly compared herself to her peers and beat herself up for even the smallest mistakes. Her perfectionism began to take a toll on her mental health, leading to chronic stress, anxiety, and burnout.

One day, after receiving a less-than-perfect grade on a paper, Jasmine had a breakdown. She realized that her pursuit of perfection was making her miserable and holding her back from living an authentic, fulfilling life. She decided it was time to make a change.

With the help of a therapist, Jasmine began to explore the roots of her perfectionism and challenge the negative beliefs and fears that fueled it. She learned to reframe her mistakes as opportunities for growth and to celebrate her progress rather than fixating on her shortcomings.

Jasmine also started practicing self-compassion and letting go of the need for external validation. She began to focus on her own values and passions rather than trying to meet others' expectations or fit into a narrow mold of success. She started pursuing activities that brought her joy and fulfillment, like painting and volunteering at a local animal shelter.

As Jasmine embraced her authentic self and let go of her perfectionism, she noticed a shift in her relationships and overall well-being. She felt more connected and genuine in her interactions with others and less burdened by the weight of constant self-criticism and doubt. She also experienced a greater sense of resilience and adaptability in the face of challenges and setbacks.

Through her journey, Jasmine learned that true self-love and acceptance means embracing all parts of herself—flaws, quirks, and all. She realized that her worth and value were not contingent on her achievements or appearance but on her inherent humanity and uniqueness. By letting go of perfectionism and embracing authenticity, Jasmine found a deeper sense of peace, purpose, and joy in her life.

Exercise 1: Reframing Negative Self-Talk

1. Take a few minutes to reflect on your inner dialogue and the common negative thoughts or beliefs that arise for you. Write down 3–5 of these negative statements, such as "I'm not good enough," "I always mess things up," or "I'll never be successful."

2. For each negative statement, ask yourself: Is this thought 100% true? Is there any evidence to the contrary? What would a kind, supportive friend say about this thought?

3. Now, rewrite each negative statement into a more balanced, compassionate, and realistic one. For example, instead of "I'm not good enough," you might write "I am doing my best and learning every day." Instead of "I always mess things up," you might write "Sometimes I make mistakes, but that doesn't define me or my worth."

4. Take a few deep breaths and repeat your reframed statements to yourself, either silently or out loud. Notice how they feel in your body and mind.

5. Choose one of your reframed statements to turn into an affirmation or mantra you can use in moments of self-doubt or criticism. Write it down somewhere you'll see it often, like on a sticky note on your mirror or as a reminder on your phone.

6. Practice repeating your affirmation to yourself daily, especially in moments when negative self-talk arises. Over time, notice how your inner dialogue begins to shift and become more self-compassionate and supportive.

The goal of this exercise is to build awareness of your negative self-talk and start to challenge and reframe it with more loving, realistic perspectives. By practicing this regularly, you can begin to rewire your inner critic and cultivate a more self-accepting and empowering mindset.

Exercise 2: Embracing Imperfection Through Creative Self-Expression

1. Choose a creative activity you enjoy but often avoid due to perfectionism or fear of judgment. This could be writing, drawing, dancing, singing, or any other form of self-expression.

2. Set aside at least 30 minutes to engage in this activity without any specific goal or outcome in mind. Give yourself permission to create freely and imperfectly.

3. As you engage in the activity, notice any thoughts or feelings that arise, especially those related to self-criticism,

comparison, or the need for perfection. Acknowledge these thoughts without judgment and then gently redirect your focus back to the process of creating.

4. If you find yourself getting stuck or frustrated, take a deep breath and remind yourself that the goal is not to create something perfect but to express yourself authentically and enjoy the process. You might even try intentionally making a "mistake" or adding an imperfect element to your creation as a way of embracing imperfection.

5. When you have finished your creative activity, take a moment to reflect on the experience. What did you notice about your inner dialogue and the thoughts and feelings that arose? What was it like to create without the pressure of perfection or external validation?

6. Consider sharing your imperfect creation with a trusted friend or family member or even posting it on social media with a caption about embracing imperfection and authenticity. Notice any feelings of vulnerability or fear that arise and practice self-compassion and courage.

The goal of this exercise is to practice letting go of perfectionism and the need for external validation through creative self-expression. By engaging in the process of creating imperfectly and vulnerably, you can start to cultivate a greater sense of self-acceptance and authenticity in all areas of your life. Remember, the goal is progress, not perfection—and every step toward embracing your true self is a step in the right direction.

Self-Reflection Questions

As you've journeyed through this chapter on overcoming barriers to self-love, you may have recognized some of your own struggles and challenges reflected in these pages. From battling negative self-talk to breaking free from perfectionism, the path to genuine self-love is rarely a straight or easy one. But by bringing awareness to these common barriers and equipping yourself with practical strategies and tools, you are already well on your way to cultivating a deeper, more compassionate relationship with yourself. To further support you in integrating these teachings and applying them to your unique experiences, I invite you to pause and reflect on the following questions. Find a quiet space, grab a journal or a trusted friend, and allow yourself to explore your answers with honesty, curiosity, and self-compassion.

1. What are some of the most persistent negative self-talk patterns or beliefs you have noticed in your inner dialogue? How have these patterns impacted your sense of self-worth and your ability to show yourself love and compassion?

2. Reflect on a time when your perfectionism or fear of failure held you back from pursuing a goal, trying something new, or expressing yourself authentically. What were the costs of this self-imposed limitation, and what might have been possible if you had been willing to embrace imperfection and take a risk?

3. Consider the relationships in your life that you would describe as "toxic" or draining. What specific behaviors or dynamics in these relationships contribute to feelings of self-doubt, insecurity, or low self-esteem? What would it look like to start setting clearer boundaries or even releasing these relationships altogether?

4. Think about a mistake or failure from your past that you still hold onto with a sense of shame, regret, or self-judgment.

How might you begin to reframe this experience as a learning opportunity or a chance for growth and self-discovery? What would it feel like to extend yourself forgiveness and compassion rather than continuing to punish yourself?

5. Identify a situation or context in which you often find yourself worrying about the judgments or opinions of others. What is at the root of this fear of judgment, and how does it hold you back from living authentically and loving yourself fully? What small steps could you take to start prioritizing your own needs, desires, and values over external validation?

6. Reflect on a challenge or obstacle you are currently facing in your self-love journey. How can you apply the strategies and insights from this chapter to support yourself in moving through this barrier with greater ease and self-compassion? What additional resources or support might you need to overcome this challenge fully?

Remember, the journey of self-love is a deeply personal and ongoing one. There is no one-size-fits-all approach or timeline for breaking through these barriers and claiming your inherent worthiness. Trust your unique process and be gentle with yourself along the way. Every moment of self-awareness and every act of self-compassion, no matter how small, is a powerful step forward on the path to radical self-love.

Your Feedback Matters!

As we wrap up Chapter 2 and embark on the final leg of our self-love journey together, I want to take a moment to express my heartfelt gratitude for your presence, engagement, and commitment to your own growth and transformation. Your willingness to show up for yourself, dive deep into the messiness and magic of self-love, and embrace the challenges and triumphs along the way has been truly inspiring to witness.

But here's the thing: As much as I've poured my heart and soul into creating this book and sharing my own experiences and insights, I know that the real magic happens when we come together as a community and learn from each other. That is why I'm reaching out to you, dear reader, to ask for your honest feedback, reflections, and insights as we close out this chapter.

Whether it is a personal anecdote that resonated with you, a lightbulb moment that shifted your perspective, or a suggestion for how to make the material even more relatable and actionable, I want to hear from you. Your feedback is invaluable to me as an author and guide and to the countless other readers who will pick up this book and embark on their own self-love revolution in the future.

So, please, don't be shy! Share your thoughts, questions, and aha moments through your review.

Scan QR code to LEAVE A REVIEW

Chapter 3:

Begin Your Path to Self-Love

So, you've decided to start this whole self-love thing. You've identified the barriers holding you back and are ready to kick them to the curb. Fantastic! Give yourself a high five because you're about to take action.

Embracing Your Authentic Self

First things first: Let's talk about authenticity. I'm not just talking about being real on Instagram (although that is important, too). I'm talking about trusting your gut, celebrating what makes you unique, and showing up as your true self in every aspect of your life.

Sounds easy, right? Well, not always. In a world that is constantly telling us who we should be, it can be tough to tune out the noise and listen to our own inner voice. But here's the thing: When you start living authentically, everything else falls into place.

How do you do it? Start by paying attention to your intuition. That little voice inside you that tells you when something feels right or wrong? Yeah, that one. Learn to trust it, even when it goes against what everyone else is saying.

Next, celebrate your quirks and imperfections. Those things that make you different? They're not flaws; they're what make you uniquely you. Embrace them, own them, and let them shine.

And finally, practice showing up as your authentic self in all areas of your life. That means being honest about your thoughts and feelings, setting boundaries when you need to, and surrounding yourself with people who love and accept you for who you are.

It might feel scary at first, but trust me: The more you practice authenticity, the more natural it becomes. Before you know it, you'll be living a life that feels true to you in every way.

Self-Acceptance: Embracing Your Flaws

Let's talk about flaws. We've all got them—those little imperfections that we wish we could change or hide or photoshop out of existence. But your flaws are not a problem to be fixed. They're a part of what makes you human, and they deserve to be accepted and even celebrated.

I know, it is easier said than done. We're so used to picking ourselves apart, focusing on all the ways we fall short of some impossible standard of perfection. But what if we flipped the script? What if, instead of trying to change our flaws, we learned to love them instead?

That is where self-acceptance comes in. It is the radical act of looking at yourself—all of yourself—and saying, "You know what? I'm okay with this. I'm okay with me."

It is not always easy, and it takes practice. One key component of self-acceptance is forgiveness. Forgiveness of others, yes, but more importantly, forgiveness of yourself. Forgiveness for not being perfect, for making mistakes, for being human.

When you learn to forgive yourself, you create space for self-acceptance to grow. You stop beating yourself up for your imperfections and start seeing them as a natural part of who you are. You start treating yourself with the same kindness and compassion you would offer a good friend.

The more you practice self-acceptance, the more you'll start to see your flaws not as weaknesses but as unique strengths and quirks that make you who you are. You'll start to appreciate your body for all the amazing things it can do rather than picking it apart for all the ways it doesn't match up to some arbitrary standard of beauty.

So, start small. Start by looking in the mirror and finding one thing you love about yourself, flaws and all. Start by practicing self-forgiveness, even when it feels hard. Start by surrounding yourself with people who accept and celebrate you, just as you are.

At the end of the day, self-acceptance is not about being perfect. It is about being perfectly imperfect and loving yourself anyway.

Self-Esteem: Building Your Inner Confidence

Now, let's talk about confidence. I'm not just talking about the kind of confidence that comes from a killer outfit or a great hair day (although those are nice, too). I'm talking about the kind of confidence that comes from deep within—the unshakable belief in your worth and value as a person.

That is self-esteem, and it is a key component of self-love. When you have high self-esteem, you trust yourself, believe in your abilities, and know that you're worthy of love and respect, no matter what.

For a lot of us, self-esteem doesn't come naturally. We've been taught to doubt ourselves, compare ourselves to others, and base our worth on external validation and approval. Over time, those messages can really do a number on our confidence.

So, how do you build your self-esteem? It starts with treating yourself like someone worth esteeming. That means talking to yourself with kindness and respect, even when you make mistakes. It means setting healthy boundaries and saying no to things that don't serve you. It means celebrating your achievements and giving yourself credit for your hard work.

It also means surrounding yourself with people and experiences that make you feel good about yourself. That might mean joining a supportive community or taking up a new hobby that brings you joy. It might mean seeking out role models and mentors who inspire you to be your best self.

Of course, it means practicing self-care and self-compassion. When you take care of yourself physically, emotionally, and mentally, you send a powerful message to yourself that you matter. You deserve to feel good, to be happy, to thrive.

Building self-esteem takes time and practice, but the payoff is so worth it. When you have a strong sense of self-worth, you show up in the world with more confidence, resilience, and joy. You're better able to handle challenges and setbacks because you know that they don't define you. You're more likely to pursue your dreams and take risks because you believe in yourself and your abilities.

Start small. Start by noticing your self-talk and replacing negative thoughts with positive ones. Start by setting small goals for yourself and celebrating when you achieve them. Start by surrounding yourself with people and experiences that make you feel good about who you are.

And remember: Your worth is not up for debate. You are valuable, you are worthy, and you deserve to feel confident and sure of yourself, always.

Self-Compassion and Forgiveness

Self-compassion is about more than just being nice. It is about treating yourself with the same kindness, understanding, and forgiveness that you would offer a good friend. It is about recognizing that you're human, and that means you're going to make mistakes, have flaws, and face challenges, just like everyone else.

Here's the thing: When you practice self-compassion, you're not just making yourself feel better in the moment. You're actually rewiring your brain to be more resilient, more adaptable, and more able to handle stress and setbacks.

How do you do it? Start by noticing when you're being hard on yourself. When you make a mistake or face a challenge, pay attention to your self-talk. Are you beating yourself up, calling yourself names, or telling yourself you're a failure? That is a sign that you need a little self-compassion.

Next, try to reframe those negative thoughts with more compassionate ones. Instead of "I'm so stupid," try "I made a mistake, but that doesn't define me." Instead of "I'm a failure," try "I'm learning and growing, and that is okay."

It might feel a little awkward at first, but the more you practice self-compassion, the more natural it becomes. The more you practice, the more you'll start to see the benefits in your life. You'll be more resilient in the face of stress and setbacks, more able to learn from your mistakes, and more able to forgive yourself and move on.

That brings us to forgiveness: forgiveness of ourselves and forgiveness of others. Because let's face it: We all make mistakes, and we all hurt people sometimes, even when we don't mean to.

However, holding onto anger, resentment, or guilt doesn't serve anyone. It just weighs us down and keeps us stuck in the past. Forgiveness, on the other hand, allows us to let go, move on, and focus on the present and the future.

Forgiveness doesn't mean condoning hurtful behavior or letting people walk all over you. It just means releasing the anger and pain that is holding you back and choosing to move forward with compassion and understanding.

When it comes to forgiving ourselves, it is even more important. Because let's face it: We're often our own harshest critics. We beat ourselves up for mistakes we made years ago or hold onto guilt and shame for things that are long past.

What if we could let that go? What if we could offer ourselves the same forgiveness and compassion that we would offer a good friend? What if we could learn from our mistakes, make amends where necessary, and then move on with our lives?

That is the power of self-compassion and forgiveness. It allows us to heal, grow, and become the best versions of ourselves. So, start small.

Start by noticing when you're being hard on yourself and practice replacing those negative thoughts with more compassionate ones. Start by offering forgiveness to yourself and others, even when it feels hard.

Remember: You are worthy of compassion and forgiveness, always. No matter what.

Setting Boundaries for Self-Respect

Setting boundaries is an act of self-love. It is a way of saying, "I matter, and my needs and desires matter, too." It is a way of showing yourself the same respect and consideration that you would show someone else.

For a lot of us, setting boundaries can be tough. We're so used to putting other people's needs before our own, saying yes to things we don't really want to do, or allowing others to cross our boundaries without consequence.

Over time, that can really take a toll on our self-respect and sense of self-worth. We start to feel like doormats, like our needs and desires don't matter, like we're not worthy of respect and consideration.

So, how do you start setting boundaries? It starts with getting clear on what you need and want. What are your values, priorities, and non-negotiables? What makes you feel good, and what makes you feel drained, stressed, or resentful?

Once you have a clear sense of your needs and desires, it is time to start communicating them to others. That might mean saying no to things that don't align with your values or priorities. It might mean setting limits on your time or energy or asking for help when you need it.

It might also mean having difficult conversations with people who are crossing your boundaries. That can be scary, but remember: You have a right to assert your needs and desires, and you deserve to be treated with respect and consideration.

And here's the thing: When you start setting boundaries, you might face some pushback or resistance from others. They might not be used to you asserting yourself, or they might feel threatened by your newfound self-respect.

But hold your ground. Remember that your boundaries are not up for negotiation and that you deserve to be treated with respect and consideration, always. Surround yourself with people who support and respect your boundaries, and let go of those who don't.

Most importantly, practice self-compassion and self-forgiveness as you navigate this process. Setting boundaries is a skill, and like any skill, it takes practice. You might make mistakes or feel guilty or selfish at times. But you're doing this for you because you matter and your needs matter.

So, start small. Start by identifying one area of your life where you need to set a boundary and practice communicating that boundary to others. Start by saying no to things that don't serve you and yes to things that do.

Remember: Setting boundaries is not selfish. It is an act of self-love and self-respect, and it is essential for your overall well-being and happiness.

Nurturing Your Body and Mind

Let's talk about self-care. And I'm not just talking about bubble baths and face masks. I'm talking about the kind of self-care that nurtures your body, mind, and soul—the kind of self-care that helps you show up as your best self in the world.

See, here's the thing: Taking care of yourself is not a luxury. It is a necessity. When you're running on empty, when you're stressed out, burnt out, and stretched too thin, you're not able to show up fully in your life. You're not able to be there for the people you love, pursue your passions and goals, or enjoy the simple pleasures of life.

When you prioritize self-care, when you make time for the things that nourish and recharge you, everything else falls into place. You have more energy, more focus, more resilience. You're able to handle stress and challenges with more ease and grace. You're able to show up as your best self in all areas of your life.

What does self-care look like? It is different for everyone, but here are a few ideas to get you started:

- Move your body in ways that feel good. That might mean going for a run, taking a yoga class, or dancing around your living room. The key is to find movement that you enjoy and that leaves you feeling energized and alive.

- Nourish your body with healthy, whole foods. That doesn't mean you have to be perfect or follow some strict diet plan. It just means paying attention to how different foods make you feel and choosing foods that leave you feeling nourished and satisfied.

- Get enough sleep. I know, easier said than done, right? However, prioritizing sleep is one of the most important things you can do for your physical and mental health. Aim for 7–9 hours a night, and create a bedtime routine that helps you wind down and relax.

- Take breaks throughout the day. Whether it is a few minutes of deep breathing, a quick walk around the block, or a full-on meditation session, taking breaks helps you recharge and refocus. It is like hitting the reset button on your brain.

- Connect with others. We're social creatures, and we need connection to thrive. Make time for the people who matter most to you, whether that is through a phone call, a coffee date, or a long hug.

- Pursue your passions and hobbies. Doing things you love, just for the sake of doing them, is a powerful form of self-care. Whether it is painting, singing, gardening, or playing an instrument, make time for the things that bring you joy and fulfillment.

- Practice mindfulness and gratitude. Taking a few minutes each day to focus on the present moment and reflect on the things you're grateful for can have a profound impact on your mental and emotional well-being. It helps you cultivate a sense of perspective and appreciation for the good things in your life.

Remember, self-care is not selfish. It is not a luxury or an indulgence. It is an essential part of taking care of yourself so you can show up fully in your life and in the world.

Where to begin? Start by incorporating one or two self-care practices into your daily routine, and notice how they make you feel. Pay attention to what nourishes and recharges you, and make time for those things, even when life gets busy.

Most importantly, remember that you are worth taking care of. You deserve to feel good, be happy, thrive. Self-care is an act of self-love and self-respect, and it is essential for your overall well-being and happiness.

So, go ahead, my friends. Nurture your body and mind in whatever ways feel good to you. You've got this.

Navigating the Ebbs and Flows of Self-Love

As you embark on your self-love journey, it is important to remember that the path is rarely linear or predictable. There will be days when you feel like you're soaring high on a wave of self-acceptance and joy and others when you feel like you're sinking back into old patterns of self-doubt and criticism.

This is completely normal and to be expected. Self-love is not a static state that we achieve once and then maintain effortlessly forever. It is a dynamic, ever-evolving relationship with ourselves that requires ongoing attention, care, and compassion.

When you find yourself in a season of struggle or setback on your self-love journey, it can be tempting to get discouraged or feel like you've failed in some way. But the truth is, these ebbs and flows are a natural part of the process. They don't mean that you're doing something wrong or that you're not making progress; they simply mean that you're human.

In fact, the moments when we feel most challenged or resistant to self-love are often the moments when we have the greatest opportunity for growth and transformation. In these times of discomfort, we're invited to dig deeper, confront the beliefs and patterns that are holding us back, and practice even greater self-compassion and patience.

So, when you find yourself in a self-love slump, remember to be extra gentle and kind with yourself. Treat yourself like you would a dear friend who is going through a tough time—with empathy, understanding, and unconditional support.

Remind yourself that this, too, shall pass and that every moment of challenge is an opportunity to strengthen your self-love muscle and develop greater resilience. Lean on your support system, whether that is a therapist, a close friend, or a self-love community, and don't be afraid to ask for help or guidance when you need it.

Most importantly, keep showing up for yourself, even when it feels hard. Keep practicing the tools and strategies that resonate with you, whether that is affirmations, journaling, meditation, or something else entirely. Trust that every small act of self-love and self-care is making a difference, even if you can't see or feel the results right away.

Remember, self-love is not about perfection or having it all figured out. It is about committing to the ongoing practice of treating yourself with kindness, compassion, and respect, no matter what life throws your way. Embrace the ebbs and flows, and know that each one is an invitation to love yourself even more deeply and fully.

Celebrating Your Self-Love Wins

On the flip side of navigating the challenges of self-love, it is equally important to celebrate and savor the moments of joy, growth, and breakthrough along the way. When you find yourself feeling particularly proud, content, or in love with yourself, take the time to really soak it in and appreciate how far you've come.

One powerful way to do this is to start a self-love wins journal or list. Each day, take a few minutes to reflect on the ways, big or small, that you practiced self-love and self-care. Maybe you set a firm boundary with a toxic friend, or you chose to prioritize your own needs over someone else's expectations. Maybe you nourished your body with a healthy meal, or you took a leap of faith and pursued a passion project.

Whatever it is, write it down and give yourself a mental high five or a physical pat on the back. Acknowledge the courage, strength, and commitment it took to choose yourself in that moment, and let yourself really feel the sense of pride and accomplishment that comes with it.

As you continue to add to your self-love wins list, you'll start to build a tangible record of your growth and progress. On days when you're feeling low or doubtful, you can look back on this list and remind yourself of all the ways you've shown up for yourself and proven your resilience and worth.

Another way to celebrate your self-love wins is to share them with others. This might mean texting a close friend about a recent breakthrough or posting about a self-care victory on social media. By sharing your wins with your community, you not only get to bask in the glow of their support and encouragement, but you also inspire others to prioritize their own self-love and self-care.

Remember, celebrating your self-love wins isn't about bragging or seeking external validation. It is about taking the time to acknowledge and appreciate the hard work and dedication you're putting into your growth and well-being. It is about reinforcing the belief that you are worthy of love, respect, and celebration, no matter what.

So, don't be shy about patting yourself on the back and doing a little happy dance when you have a self-love win. Embrace the joy and pride that comes with treating yourself with love and care, and let it fuel you forward on your ongoing journey.

Who knows? Your self-love wins might just be the very thing that someone else needs to see or hear to inspire them on their own path. By shining your light and celebrating your own growth, you create a ripple effect of love and positivity that extends far beyond yourself.

Case Study: Cultivating Self-Love in Action

Meet Elena, a 28-year-old graphic designer who had always struggled with self-doubt and people-pleasing tendencies. Despite her talent and success in her career, Elena often felt like an imposter, constantly seeking external validation and approval from others.

Elena's turning point came when she was passed over for a promotion at work despite having worked countless hours of overtime and sacrificed her personal life for the company. The rejection hit her hard, and she realized that she had been pouring all of her energy into pleasing others while neglecting her own needs and desires.

Determined to make a change, Elena embarked on a journey of self-love and self-discovery. She started by setting aside time each day for activities that brought her joy and fulfillment, like painting and hiking in nature. She also began practicing self-compassion, learning to treat herself with kindness and understanding, even in the face of setbacks or mistakes.

As Elena continued to prioritize her own well-being, she noticed a shift in her relationships and work life. She began setting healthy boundaries with colleagues and friends, saying no to requests that didn't align with her values or goals. She also started speaking up more in meetings and advocating for her ideas rather than constantly deferring to others.

Through her self-love practice, Elena cultivated a deeper sense of authenticity and confidence. She no longer felt the need to seek external validation or approval because she had learned to validate and approve of herself. She also found that she was able to show up more fully and genuinely in her relationships, attracting people who appreciated and supported her true self.

While Elena's self-love journey was not always easy, she remained committed to nurturing her mind, body, and soul. She learned to embrace her flaws and imperfections, seeing them as unique parts of her identity rather than weaknesses to be fixed. She also developed a greater sense of resilience and adaptability, knowing she had the inner strength and resources to handle whatever challenges came her way.

Through her experience, Elena discovered that self-love is not a destination but a lifelong practice. By making small, consistent choices to prioritize her well-being and authenticity, she was able to transform her life and relationships in profound ways. She now shares her story with others, inspiring them to embark on their own self-love journeys and cultivate a deeper sense of joy, purpose, and fulfillment.

Exercise 1: Cultivating Self-Compassion Through Letter Writing

1. Imagine that a close friend or loved one is going through a difficult time and has come to you for support. They are struggling with feelings of inadequacy, self-doubt, and shame.

2. Take out a piece of paper and a pen, and write a letter to this person, offering them the same compassion, understanding, and encouragement you would want to receive in a similar situation.

3. In your letter, acknowledge your friend's struggles and validate their feelings. Remind them of their inherent worth and value and the qualities and strengths that make them unique and special.

4. Offer words of support and encouragement, reminding your friend that mistakes and setbacks are a normal part of the human experience and that they have the resilience and capability to overcome challenges and grow from them.

5. Now, take a moment to reread the letter, imagining that the words of compassion and encouragement are being directed toward yourself. Notice any feelings of resistance or discomfort that arise and gently acknowledge them without judgment.

6. As you reread the letter, replace your friend's name with your own, personalizing the message of self-compassion and support. Allow yourself to fully receive and absorb the words of kindness and understanding.

7. Reflect on how it feels to extend the same level of compassion and encouragement to yourself as you would to a loved one. Notice any shifts in your mood, mindset, or self-talk.

8. Consider making this letter-writing practice a regular part of your self-love routine, either by writing to yourself or exchanging letters of compassion with a trusted friend or family member.

The goal of this exercise is to cultivate a deeper sense of self-compassion and kindness, recognizing that we all deserve the same level of love, support, and understanding that we so readily extend to others. By practicing self-compassion through letter writing, we can begin to internalize a more loving and accepting relationship with ourselves.

Exercise 2: Nurturing Your Mind and Body Through Mindful Self-Care

1. Take a few moments to check in with yourself and notice any areas of tension, discomfort, or unmet needs in your mind and body. Without judgment, simply observe and acknowledge what you are experiencing.

2. Create a list of self-care activities that nourish and support your physical, emotional, and mental well-being. These might include things like taking a warm bath, practicing yoga or stretching, reading a book, spending time in nature, or enjoying a favorite hobby.

3. Choose one activity from your list that you feel drawn to in this moment and set aside at least 20–30 minutes to fully engage in it without distractions or interruptions.

4. As you engage in your chosen self-care activity, practice being fully present and mindful. Notice any sensations, thoughts, or emotions that arise without getting caught up in them or trying to change them.

5. If your mind starts to wander or get distracted, gently bring your attention back to the present moment and the activity at hand. Remind yourself that this time is a gift to yourself and an act of self-love and self-care.

6. When you have finished your self-care activity, take a few moments to reflect on the experience. Notice any changes in your mood, energy level, or overall sense of well-being.

7. Consider making mindful self-care a regular part of your daily or weekly routine, even if it is just for a few minutes at a time.

Experiment with different activities and practices to find what works best for you and your unique needs.

8. Remember that self-care is not a luxury or indulgence but an essential part of maintaining your physical, emotional, and mental health. By nurturing your mind and body through mindful self-care, you are sending a powerful message of love and respect to yourself.

The goal of this exercise is to cultivate a deeper sense of self-awareness and self-care, recognizing that taking care of ourselves is not selfish but a necessary part of living a healthy, fulfilling life. By practicing mindful self-care, we can learn to tune in to our needs and desires and respond to them with compassion and care. Over time, this practice can help to build greater resilience, self-esteem, and overall well-being.

Self-Reflection Questions

As you've explored the various practices and strategies for beginning your self-love journey in this chapter, you may have felt a mix of excitement, inspiration, and perhaps even some discomfort or resistance. That is totally normal—embarking on a path of deeper self-love and self-acceptance is a brave and transformative choice, but it is not always an easy one. It requires us to confront old patterns, beliefs, and fears and to step outside of our comfort zones in service of our growth and healing. But as you've seen through the stories and examples shared, the rewards of this work are truly immeasurable—from greater authenticity and confidence to more fulfilling relationships and a deeper sense of purpose and joy. To support you in integrating and personalizing these teachings, I invite you to carve out some time for reflection, either on your own or with a trusted friend or journal. Allow yourself to explore the following questions with curiosity, honesty, and self-compassion, trusting that whatever arises is a valuable part of your unique self-love journey.

1. Reflect on a time when you felt truly authentic and aligned with your deepest self. What were you doing? Who were you with? How did it feel in your body and mind? What can you learn from this experience about what authenticity means to you?

2. What are some of the ways you tend to hold yourself back from fully showing up as your authentic self—whether in your relationships, your work, or your creative pursuits? What fears, doubts, or limiting beliefs arise when you imagine letting go of these barriers and living more authentically?

3. Identify one or two of your perceived flaws or imperfections that you tend to judge or criticize most harshly. How might your relationship with these parts of yourself shift if you approached them with more acceptance, compassion, and even appreciation?

4. Think about an area of your life where you feel a lack of confidence or low self-esteem. What experiences, messages, or beliefs have contributed to this sense of self-doubt? What would it look like to start building a more solid foundation of inner confidence and self-trust in this area?

5. When you think about your relationship with forgiveness—both of yourself and others—what challenges or blocks arise? What might be possible in your life and relationships if you were able to approach mistakes and hurts with more forgiveness and self-compassion?

6. Reflect on your current self-care practices and rhythms. Are there any areas of your physical, emotional, mental, or spiritual well-being that feel neglected or out of balance? What are one or two simple, nourishing practices you could begin incorporating into your daily routine to support yourself more fully?

7. As you look ahead on your self-love journey, what does your most authentic, joyful, self-loving life look like? How does it feel in your mind, body, and spirit? What are some of the qualities, experiences, and relationships you want to cultivate more of as you continue on this path?

Remember, there is no single roadmap or timeline for this journey. What matters most is your willingness to keep showing up for yourself with honesty, compassion, and a beginner's mind. Trust that every moment of self-reflection, every act of self-care, and every courageous step toward your most authentic life is planting seeds that will blossom in ways you can't even imagine yet. Be patient with your progress, celebrate the small victories along the way, and know that you are worthy of your own unconditional love and acceptance, today and always.

Chapter 4:

Embracing Self-Love in the Modern World

We've covered a lot of ground so far in our exploration of self-love. We've talked about the importance of authenticity, self-acceptance, self-esteem, self-compassion, boundaries, and self-care. But let's be real: Practicing self-love in today's fast-paced, digitally driven world can feel like a whole new ballgame.

In this chapter, we're going to dive into some of the unique challenges and opportunities that come with embracing self-love in the modern world. We'll explore how to prioritize self-care when you're busy as hell, how to navigate the wild world of social media without losing yourself in the process, and how to use technology as a tool for self-love rather than a source of stress and anxiety.

We'll also touch on the importance of financial self-care in the digital economy because let's face it—money matters, and taking care of your financial health is a crucial aspect of overall self-love and well-being.

It is time to get real about what it means to love yourself in a world that is constantly telling you you're not enough. Let's do this.

Too Busy for Self-Care? Squeezing Self-Care Into a Packed Schedule

First things first, let's address the elephant in the room: time. As women in the modern world, it can often feel like there's just not enough of it to go around. We're juggling careers, families, friendships, and a million other responsibilities, all while trying to keep up with the latest trends and look effortlessly put-together in the process.

It is no wonder that self-care often falls by the wayside. When you're constantly running from one thing to the next, taking even a few minutes for yourself can feel like a luxury. But here's the thing: self-care isn't a luxury. It is a necessity.

Think about it this way: You wouldn't skip filling up your car with gas because you were too busy, right? You know that without fuel, your car won't run, and you won't be able to get where you need to go. Well, the same is true for your body and mind. Without regular self-care, you'll eventually run out of steam, and everything else in your life will suffer as a result.

So, how do you make time for self-care when your schedule is packed to the brim? Here are a few tips:

- Set clear boundaries. Learn to say no to things that don't serve you, and don't be afraid to delegate tasks when possible. Remember, you can't pour from an empty cup.

- Make self-care a priority. Treat it like any other important appointment or commitment in your life. Put it on your calendar, and protect that time fiercely.

- Look for small, manageable ways to incorporate self-care into your daily routine. This might mean taking a few deep breaths between meetings, doing a quick stretch at your desk, or savoring your morning coffee without distractions.

- Focus on quality over quantity. A ten-minute meditation or a quick walk around the block can be just as beneficial as a long yoga class or a day at the spa. The key is to be fully present and engaged in whatever self-care activity you choose.

Remember, self-care isn't selfish. It is a vital part of showing up as your best self in the world. So, start small, and start today. Your future self will thank you.

But let's dive a little deeper into this idea of setting boundaries. It is easy to say, "Learn to say no," but in practice, it can be a lot harder, especially if you're someone who tends to put others' needs before your own.

One helpful exercise is to make a list of your non-negotiables—the things that are absolutely essential to your well-being and happiness. This might include things like getting enough sleep, eating nourishing foods, spending quality time with loved ones, or pursuing a hobby that brings you joy.

Once you have your list of non-negotiables, use it as a guide for making decisions about how to spend your time and energy. If something doesn't align with your non-negotiables, it is okay to say no, even if it means disappointing someone else.

Another important aspect of setting boundaries is communicating them clearly and consistently to others. This might mean having a conversation with your boss about your workload and capacity or telling a friend that you need some alone time to recharge.

It can be scary to assert your needs and boundaries, especially if you're not used to doing so. But remember, setting boundaries is an act of self-love and self-respect. It is about honoring yourself and your needs and trusting that the right people will understand and support you.

Of course, setting boundaries is just one piece of the self-care puzzle. Another important aspect is developing a self-care routine that works for you and your lifestyle.

This might mean carving out time each day for a specific self-care activity, like journaling or taking a bath. It might mean finding ways to incorporate self-care into your existing routine, like listening to a favorite podcast while you commute or doing a few stretches before bed.

The key is to experiment and find what works for you. What feels nourishing and rejuvenating for one person might not work for another, and that is okay. The important thing is to make self-care a non-negotiable part of your daily life, even if it looks different from day to day.

One helpful way to make self-care a habit is to start small and build from there. Set a goal to do one small self-care activity each day, like taking a few deep breaths or savoring a cup of tea without distractions. As you start to feel the benefits of these small acts of self-care, you'll naturally want to incorporate more of them into your life.

Another important aspect of self-care is learning to listen to your body and mind. This means paying attention to your energy levels, emotions, and physical sensations and adjusting your self-care practices accordingly.

For example, if you're feeling physically exhausted, a high-intensity workout might not be the best form of self-care for you in that moment. Instead, you might opt for a gentle yoga class or a short walk outside to clear your head.

Similarly, if you're feeling emotionally drained, you might need a different kind of self-care than if you're feeling anxious or restless. This might mean taking a break from social media, journaling about your feelings, or reaching out to a trusted friend for support.

The key is to approach self-care with curiosity and self-compassion rather than trying to force yourself into a one-size-fits-all routine. Remember, self-care is about nourishing yourself on a deep, holistic level, not just going through the motions or checking things off a list.

And finally, it is important to remember that self-care isn't always easy or comfortable. Sometimes, the most important forms of self-care are the ones that challenge us or push us outside our comfort zones, like setting boundaries, having difficult conversations, or facing our fears.

When we approach these challenges with a spirit of self-love and self-compassion, we build resilience and strength that serve us in all areas of our lives. We learn to trust ourselves and our instincts and to show up for ourselves even when it is hard.

So, as you navigate the challenges and opportunities of practicing self-care in a busy, modern world, remember this: You are worth the time and effort it takes to care for yourself. Your needs and desires matter, and you deserve to prioritize them, even when it feels hard or uncomfortable.

Keep showing up for yourself, keep exploring what self-care looks like for you, and keep believing in your inherent worth and value. The world needs more women who love themselves fiercely and unapologetically, and that starts with you.

Digital Self-Love: Balancing Online Presence With Real Self-Worth

Alright, let's talk about the big, bad world of social media. On one hand, platforms like Instagram and Twitter can be incredible tools for connection, creativity, and self-expression. On the other hand, they can also be breeding grounds for comparison, self-doubt, and FOMO (that is "fear of missing out," for those of you who aren't hip to the lingo).

How do you navigate this digital landscape in a way that supports your self-love journey rather than undermining it? Here are a few ideas:

- Curate your feed. Follow accounts that inspire and uplift you, and don't be afraid to unfollow or mute those that make you feel bad about yourself.

- Set boundaries around your social media use. This might mean designating specific times of day for checking your feeds or taking regular breaks from social media altogether.

- Remember that what you see online is often a highlight reel, not the full picture. Everyone has struggles and insecurities, even if they don't show them on Instagram.

- Use social media as a tool for connection and community rather than just a platform for self-promotion. Engage with others genuinely and authentically, and focus on building real relationships rather than just racking up likes and followers.

- Balance your online presence with real-world experiences and connections. Make time for face-to-face conversations, hobbies that don't involve a screen, and activities that bring you joy and fulfillment.

At the end of the day, your self-worth isn't measured by your follower count or your likes. It comes from within, and it is up to you to cultivate it through self-love and self-care.

But let's be real: In today's digital age, it can be all too easy to get caught up in the highlight reel of social media and start comparing ourselves to others. We see carefully curated images of perfect bodies, perfect relationships, perfect careers, and it is easy to start feeling like we're falling short in comparison.

That is why it is so important to cultivate a strong sense of self-worth that is rooted in your own values and beliefs rather than external validation. This means taking the time to get to know yourself on a deep level—your strengths, passions, and unique quirks and qualities.

It also means learning to recognize and challenge the negative self-talk that can arise when we spend too much time scrolling through social media. When you catch yourself thinking things like "I'll never be as successful/thin/popular as her," take a step back and ask yourself if that thought is really true or if it is just a product of comparison and self-doubt.

Another helpful strategy is to actively seek out content and communities that align with your values and support your self-love journey. This might mean following body-positive influencers, joining online support groups for mental health or personal growth, or engaging with creators who inspire you and make you feel good about yourself.

But remember, even the most positive and uplifting online communities can't replace the importance of real-world connections and experiences. Make sure to balance your online presence with plenty of offline activities that bring you joy and fulfillment, whether that is spending time in nature, pursuing a creative hobby, or connecting with loved ones face-to-face.

When you do choose to engage with social media, do so with intention and mindfulness. Before you post something, ask yourself why you're sharing it and what message you want to convey. Are you posting from a place of authenticity and self-expression, or are you seeking external validation and approval?

Similarly, when you're scrolling through your feeds, notice how different types of content make you feel. If something inspires and uplifts you, great! But if it triggers feelings of comparison, self-doubt, or FOMO, it might be time to take a step back and reevaluate your relationship with that content.

Ultimately, the key to balancing your online presence with real self-worth is to approach social media with a spirit of self-awareness and self-compassion. Remember that you are so much more than your online persona and that your worth and value come from within, not from external validation.

So, go ahead and curate that Instagram feed, join that online community, and share your authentic self with the world. But always remember to prioritize your offline life and relationships and to cultivate a strong sense of self-love and self-worth that is rooted in your own values and beliefs. At the end of the day, that is what truly matters.

Technological Tools for Self-Love

Now, I know what some of you might be thinking: *Technology is the problem, not the solution! How can I use it to support my self-love journey?* I get it. Technology can be a double-edged sword, especially when it comes to mental health and well-being.

But here's the thing: When used mindfully and intentionally, technology can actually be an incredible tool for self-love and personal growth. There are countless apps, platforms, and resources out there designed specifically to support your mental health, emotional well-being, and self-care practices.

For example, there are meditation apps like Headspace and Calm that can help you develop a daily mindfulness practice, even if you only have a few minutes to spare. There are mood-tracking apps like Daylio and Moodnotes that can help you identify patterns in your emotions and behaviors and develop strategies for managing stress and anxiety.

There are also online communities and support groups for just about every topic under the sun, from mental health to body positivity to career development. These digital spaces can provide a sense of connection and belonging, especially if you don't have access to in-person support or resources.

Of course, it is important to use these tools in a way that feels healthy and balanced for you. That might mean setting limits on your screen time or being mindful of the types of content you consume online. But when used with intention and self-awareness, technology can be a powerful ally in your self-love journey.

One of the great things about technological tools for self-love is that they can be customized to fit your individual needs and preferences. Whether you're looking for guided meditations, journaling prompts, or stress-relief techniques, there's an app or platform out there that can help.

For example, if you're someone who struggles with negative self-talk or self-criticism, you might find it helpful to use an app like ThinkUp, which allows you to record and listen to positive affirmations in your own voice. Or, if you're looking for a more creative outlet for self-expression, you might enjoy using a digital art app like Procreate or Adobe Fresco to create visual representations of your thoughts and feelings.

Another benefit of technological tools for self-love is that they can help you track your progress and celebrate your successes along the way. Many apps and platforms offer features like goal-setting, habit-tracking, and progress monitoring, which can be a great way to stay motivated and accountable in your self-love journey.

For example, if one of your self-love goals is to develop a consistent gratitude practice, you might use an app like Gratitude Journal or Happyfeed to record three things you're grateful for each day. Over time, you can look back on your entries and see how far you've come in cultivating a more positive and appreciative mindset.

Of course, as with any tool, it is important to use technology mindfully and in moderation. It is easy to get caught up in the constant stream of notifications, alerts, and updates and to start relying on external validation from likes and comments.

That is why it is so important to approach technological tools for self-love with a spirit of intention and self-awareness. Before you download that app or join that online community, ask yourself what you hope to gain from it and how it aligns with your overall self-love goals.

And remember, technological tools are just that: tools. They're not a replacement for the hard work of self-reflection, self-compassion, and self-care. But when used in conjunction with those practices, they can be a powerful support system in your self-love journey.

Go ahead and experiment with different apps, platforms, and resources that resonate with you. But always remember to prioritize your own inner wisdom and intuition and to use technology as a supplement to rather than a substitute for your own self-love practices.

Financial Self-Care in the Digital Economy

Last but not least, let's talk about money. I know, I know—it is not the most glamorous topic. However, financial self-care is a crucial aspect of overall self-love and well-being, especially in today's digital economy.

With the rise of online shopping, mobile banking, and digital currencies, it is easier than ever to lose track of your spending and fall into financial stress and anxiety. But just like any other aspect of self-care, financial self-care is all about developing healthy habits and making intentional choices that align with your values and goals.

Here are a few tips for practicing financial self-care in the modern world:

- Educate yourself. Take the time to learn about personal finance, budgeting, and investing. There are tons of free resources online, from blogs to podcasts to courses.

- Create a budget. Track your income and expenses and make a plan for how you want to allocate your money each month. Don't forget to include room for self-care and fun!

- Set financial goals. Whether it is paying off debt, saving for a big purchase, or building an emergency fund, having clear financial goals can help you stay motivated and on track.

- Practice mindful spending. Before making a purchase, ask yourself if it aligns with your values and goals. Is it something you truly need or want, or are you just buying it out of habit or impulse?

- Don't be afraid to ask for help. If you're struggling with financial stress or anxiety, there's no shame in seeking support from a financial advisor, therapist, or trusted friend or family member.

Remember, financial self-care isn't about depriving yourself or living a life of scarcity. It is about making intentional choices that support your overall well-being and allow you to live a life that feels authentic and fulfilling.

One of the biggest challenges of financial self-care in the digital age is the constant bombardment of targeted ads and marketing messages. Everywhere we turn, there's someone trying to sell us something, whether it is a new gadget, a trendy fashion item, or a "life-changing" course or program.

It is easy to get swept up in the hype and start believing that we need these things to be happy, successful, or fulfilled. But the truth is, these purchases are usually just a temporary Band-Aid for deeper issues of self-worth and self-esteem.

That is why it is so important to approach financial self-care with a spirit of mindfulness and self-awareness. Before making a purchase, take a moment to check in with yourself and ask: "Why do I want this? How will it contribute to my overall well-being and happiness? Is it aligned with my values and goals?"

If the answer is no, or if you're not sure, it might be worth pressing pause on that purchase and exploring the underlying emotions or motivations behind it. Are you feeling anxious, stressed, or unfulfilled in some area of your life? Are you looking for external validation or approval? Are you trying to fill a void with material possessions?

By getting curious about these deeper issues, you can start to develop a more intentional and empowered relationship with money and spending. You can start to make choices that reflect your true values and priorities rather than just reacting to external pressures and influences.

Another important aspect of financial self-care in the digital age is learning to navigate the world of online banking and digital transactions with security and savvy. With the rise of cyber threats and identity theft, protecting your financial information and assets is more important than ever.

Some basic tips for staying safe online include using strong, unique passwords for all your accounts, being cautious about sharing personal information over email or social media, and monitoring your credit reports and bank statements regularly for any suspicious activity.

It is also a good idea to educate yourself about common scams and fraud tactics, such as phishing emails, fake job postings, and "get rich quick" schemes. Remember, if something sounds too good to be true, it probably is.

Beyond just protecting yourself from external threats, financial self-care in the digital age also means taking proactive steps to build your financial literacy and confidence. This might mean seeking out resources and tools to help you budget, save, and invest more effectively or working with a financial coach or advisor to develop a personalized plan for your unique goals and circumstances.

It might also mean challenging some of the limiting beliefs and narratives you've internalized about money and success. For example, if you've always believed that you're "bad with money" or that financial stability is out of reach for you, it might be time to question those assumptions and start building a more empowered and abundant mindset.

One powerful way to do this is through affirmations and visualization practices. By regularly affirming your financial goals and visualizing yourself achieving them, you can start to shift your subconscious beliefs and attract more opportunities and abundance into your life.

Another helpful practice is gratitude. By focusing on the things you already have and appreciate in your life, rather than constantly striving for more, you can cultivate a sense of contentment and sufficiency that supports your overall financial well-being.

Ultimately, financial self-care in the digital age is about developing a healthy, intentional, and empowered relationship with money and spending. It is about aligning your financial choices with your values and goals and using technology and resources in a way that supports your overall well-being and happiness.

Educate yourself, set those budgets and goals, and practice mindful spending. However, always remember that your bank account or credit score does not determine your worth and value as a person. True financial self-care is about creating a life of abundance, joy, and purpose, regardless of your income or circumstances.

Embracing Self-Love in the Modern World

From navigating the world of social media to using technology as a tool for self-care to practicing financial self-love in the digital economy, there's no shortage of challenges and opportunities when it comes to embracing self-love in the modern world.

But no matter how much the world changes, the core principles of self-love remain the same. It is about treating yourself with kindness, compassion, and respect. It is about setting boundaries, practicing self-care, and surrounding yourself with people and experiences that lift you up and support your growth.

Most importantly, it is about remembering that you are worthy of love and belonging, just as you are. No matter what your social media feed says, no matter what your bank account says, no matter what society says, you are enough, and you deserve to be loved and cared for.

So, keep doing the work, my friends. Keep showing up for yourself, even when it is hard. Keep learning and growing and exploring what self-love looks like for you. Keep believing in yourself and your inherent worth and value.

The world needs more people who love themselves fully and unapologetically. The world needs more people who are willing to stand up for themselves, speak their truth, and live a life that feels authentic and fulfilling to them.

And that all starts with you. So, go out there and love yourself like your life depends on it because, in a way, it does.

But let's be real: Embracing self-love in the modern world is not always easy. There will be days when you fall into the comparison trap on social media, when you overspend on an impulse purchase, or when you neglect your self-care in the face of a busy schedule.

And that is okay. Self-love is not about perfection; it is about progress. It is about showing up for yourself with compassion and understanding, even when you stumble or fall short of your own expectations.

It is also about recognizing that self-love is not a one-time achievement but a lifelong practice. Just like any other skill or habit, it requires ongoing effort, commitment, and dedication.

The good news is every small step you take toward self-love is a step in the right direction. Every time you choose to prioritize your own needs and well-being, every time you set a healthy boundary or practice self-compassion, and every time you surround yourself with positive and uplifting influences, you are strengthening your self-love muscle and creating a more fulfilling and authentic life for yourself.

The even better news is you don't have to do it alone. There are countless resources, communities, and support systems out there to help you on your self-love journey—whether it is a therapist or coach, an online group or forum, a trusted friend or family member, or a self-help book or program.

The key is to seek out the resources and support that resonate with you and your unique needs and goals. There is no one-size-fits-all approach to self-love, and what works for someone else may not work for you, and that is okay.

The most important thing is to keep exploring, experimenting, and showing up for yourself with curiosity, compassion, and a willingness to learn and grow.

And remember, self-love is not just about feeling good in the moment; it is about creating a life that feels authentic, fulfilling, and joyful in the long run. It is about building resilience, cultivating inner peace and contentment, and showing up as your best self in all areas of your life.

Practicing Radical Self-Acceptance in a Filtered World

In today's digital age, it is easy to get caught up in the pressure to present a perfect, polished version of ourselves to the world. From carefully curated social media feeds to the abundance of filters and editing tools at our fingertips, we are constantly bombarded with images of airbrushed perfection that can make us feel like our own lives and appearances are falling short.

However, the truth is that no amount of external validation or digital manipulation can replace the power of true self-acceptance. Radical self-acceptance means embracing yourself fully, flaws and all, and recognizing that your worth is not dependent on your appearance, achievements, or social media likes.

Practicing radical self-acceptance in a filtered world starts with recognizing the ways in which you may be internalizing harmful beauty standards and unrealistic expectations. Notice when you find yourself comparing your own life or appearance to others online, and gently remind yourself that what you see is often a highlight reel, not the full picture.

Instead of striving for perfection, try shifting your focus to self-compassion and authenticity. Embrace your unique quirks, imperfections, and experiences as part of what makes you beautifully human. Practice speaking to yourself with the same kindness and understanding you would offer a beloved friend, and surround yourself with people and content that celebrate diversity and encourage self-love.

Another powerful way to cultivate radical self-acceptance is to focus on gratitude and appreciation for your body and all the amazing things it allows you to do. Instead of fixating on perceived flaws or areas you wish to change, try thanking your body for its strength, resilience, and ability to carry you through life's challenges and joys.

You might also try engaging in practices that promote self-acceptance and body positivity, such as mirror work, intuitive movement, or creative self-expression. By learning to love and appreciate yourself exactly as you are, you can begin to let go of the need for external validation and find a deeper sense of peace and contentment within.

Remember, radical self-acceptance is not about settling or giving up on personal growth and self-improvement. It is about recognizing that you are already inherently worthy and deserving of love and respect, regardless of your appearance or accomplishments. By practicing self-acceptance in a filtered world, you can cultivate a more authentic and empowered sense of self that radiates from the inside out.

Nurturing Slow Living and Mindfulness in a Fast-Paced World

In today's fast-paced, technology-driven world, getting caught up in the constant hustle and grind of productivity and achievement is easy. We are often so focused on checking off our to-do lists, keeping up with the latest trends and information, and optimizing every moment of our day that we forget to slow down and savor the present moment.

However, the practice of slow living and mindfulness can be a powerful antidote to the stress and overwhelm of modern life. By intentionally slowing down and bringing our full attention to the present moment, we can cultivate a greater sense of peace, joy, and connection to ourselves and the world around us.

Nurturing slow living and mindfulness starts with recognizing how you may be operating on autopilot or constantly rushing from one thing to the next. Notice when you find yourself multitasking, checking your phone compulsively, or feeling anxious about the future, and take a moment to pause and reconnect with the present.

One simple way to incorporate mindfulness into your daily life is to practice deep breathing or meditation, even if only for a few minutes a day. By focusing on your breath and observing your thoughts and sensations without judgment, you can begin to cultivate a greater sense of calm and clarity.

You might also try incorporating more slow, intentional activities into your routine, such as savoring a cup of tea without distractions, taking a leisurely walk in nature, or engaging in a creative hobby that allows you to lose track of time and enter a state of flow.

Another key aspect of slow living is learning to let go of the pressure to constantly be productive or optimize every moment. Give yourself permission to rest, play, and simply be without feeling guilty or unproductive. Recognize that taking time for self-care and enjoyment is not a luxury but a necessary part of a balanced and fulfilling life.

Mindfulness can also be a powerful tool for cultivating self-love and self-compassion. By learning to observe your thoughts and emotions with curiosity and non-judgment, you can begin to let go of harsh self-criticism and embrace a more kind and accepting relationship with yourself.

Remember, nurturing slow living and mindfulness is not about completely overhauling your life or retreating from the world. It is about finding small, sustainable ways to bring more presence, intention, and self-care into your daily routines and interactions.

By embracing the power of mindfulness and slow living, you can begin to find a greater sense of balance, peace, and joy amidst the chaos of modern life. You can cultivate a more loving and compassionate relationship with yourself and others and create a life that feels more authentic, fulfilling, and true to your deepest values and desires.

Case Study: Navigating Self-Love in the Digital Age

Meet Sophia, a 32-year-old social media manager who had always prided herself on her online presence and digital savvy. With thousands of followers across multiple platforms, Sophia spent countless hours curating the perfect feed, engaging with her audience, and staying on top of the latest trends and algorithms.

Despite her success in the digital world, Sophia often felt a nagging sense of emptiness and disconnection. She found herself constantly comparing her life to the highlight reels of others and feeling like she was never quite measuring up. She also struggled with setting boundaries around her social media use, often sacrificing sleep, self-care, and real-world connections in favor of online engagement.

One day, after a particularly draining week of online drama and comparison, Sophia reached a breaking point. She realized that her pursuit of digital perfection was taking a toll on her mental health and overall well-being. She knew that something needed to change.

With the help of a therapist and a supportive group of friends, Sophia began to explore self-love and authenticity in the context of her digital life. She started by unfollowing accounts that triggered feelings of inadequacy or comparison and seeking out content that inspired and uplifted her instead.

Sophia also began to set clearer boundaries around her social media use, designating specific times of day for checking her feeds and engaging with her audience. She made a conscious effort to prioritize offline activities and connections, like hiking with friends or taking a pottery class, as a way to balance out her digital life.

As Sophia continued to practice self-love and self-care in the digital age, she noticed a shift in her online presence as well. She began to share more authentic and vulnerable content, opening up about her struggles and imperfections rather than just presenting a curated highlight reel. She also started using her platform to spread messages of self-love, body positivity, and mental health awareness.

To her surprise, Sophia found that her audience responded positively to her more authentic and empowered approach. She received messages from followers thanking her for her honesty and vulnerability and sharing their own struggles and triumphs with self-love in the digital age.

Through her journey, Sophia learned that true self-love and authenticity in the modern world require a delicate balance of online and offline connection, intentional boundary-setting, and a commitment to prioritizing one's own well-being above external validation or approval.

She also discovered the power of using digital tools and platforms to support, rather than undermine, her self-love journey. By seeking out uplifting content, engaging in supportive online communities, and using technology to enhance her self-care practices, Sophia was able to cultivate a more positive and empowered relationship with both her digital and real-world selves.

While navigating self-love in the digital age is an ongoing process, Sophia now approaches it with a greater sense of agency, intention, and self-compassion. She recognizes that her worth and value come from within, not from her follower count or online persona, and she is committed to using her platform and presence to reflect her authentic self and uplift others on their self-love journeys.

Exercise 1: Digital Detox Challenge

1. Choose a specific period of time for your digital detox, whether it is a few hours, a day, or a weekend. Commit to completely unplugging from all social media, email, and non-essential digital communication during this time.

2. Before beginning your detox, take a few minutes to set an intention for how you want to spend your time offline. What activities or experiences do you want to prioritize? What aspects of your self-care or personal growth do you want to focus on?

3. Let key people in your life know about your digital detox plan so they can support you and know not to expect an immediate response during this time.

4. Once your detox begins, notice any feelings of discomfort, anxiety, or FOMO that arise. Acknowledge these feelings

without judgment, and remind yourself that they are temporary and a normal part of the detox process.

5. Fill your detox time with nourishing offline activities, such as reading a book, taking a bath, going for a walk in nature, engaging in a creative hobby, or connecting with loved ones face-to-face.

6. If you find yourself reaching for your phone or tempted to check social media out of habit, take a deep breath and redirect your attention to the present moment. Engage your senses by noticing your surroundings, taking a few mindful breaths, or savoring a cup of tea.

7. At the end of your detox period, take some time to reflect on the experience. What did you notice about your relationship with technology and social media? How did it feel to unplug and focus on offline activities and connections? What, if anything, do you want to change about your digital habits moving forward?

8. Consider incorporating regular digital detox practices into your self-care routine, whether it is a weekly social media-free day or a nightly phone-free hour before bed.

The goal of this exercise is to create space for self-reflection, self-care, and real-world connection away from the constant stimulation and comparison of the digital world. By taking intentional breaks from technology, we can cultivate a more mindful and balanced relationship with it and prioritize our own well-being and authenticity both online and off.

Exercise 2: Aligning Your Online Presence With Your Authentic Self

1. Take a few minutes to reflect on your current online presence across various social media platforms. What kind of content do you typically post? What persona or image do you project to your followers?

2. Now, take a moment to connect with your authentic self. What are your core values, passions, and beliefs? What aspects of your identity and experience do you want to share more of online?

3. Make a list of 3–5 ways you can align your online presence more closely with your authentic self. This might include sharing more vulnerable or personal stories, posting content that reflects your true interests and passions, or using your platform to advocate for causes you care about.

4. Choose one item from your list to focus on this week. Set a specific goal for how you will incorporate this authentic element into your online presence, whether it is sharing a certain type of post, engaging in a meaningful conversation, or updating your bio to reflect your true self.

5. As you begin to implement this change, notice any fears, doubts, or resistance that arise. Acknowledge these feelings with self-compassion, and remind yourself that authenticity is a process of gradual unfolding, not an overnight transformation.

6. Seek out support and inspiration from others who are committed to authentic living and self-love, both online and off. Follow accounts that align with your values and make you

feel seen and understood. Engage in meaningful conversations and connections with like-minded individuals.

7. Regularly check in with yourself about how your online presence feels in relation to your authentic self. Are there any areas where you still feel misaligned or inauthentic? What small steps can you take to continue bringing your true self to your digital interactions?

8. Celebrate your progress and courage in showing up more authentically online. Remember that your vulnerability and realness are a gift to yourself and others and that your worth and value are not determined by external validation or approval.

The goal of this exercise is to cultivate a more authentic and aligned online presence that reflects your true self and values. By bringing more of our real selves to our digital interactions, we create space for genuine connection, self-expression, and the kind of vulnerability that fosters true self-love and acceptance. While it may feel risky or uncomfortable at first, aligning our online presence with our authentic selves is a powerful way to practice self-love and create a more fulfilling and meaningful digital life.

Self-Reflection Questions

As you've read through this chapter on embracing self-love in the modern world, you may have encountered some familiar challenges and discovered new insights about navigating the digital landscape with authenticity and intention. From the constant demands on your time and energy to the pressure to present a curated image online, the obstacles to self-love in today's fast-paced, technology-driven culture are real and pervasive. However, by bringing mindfulness and self-awareness to your relationship with technology, social media, and financial well-being, you have the power to transform these potential pitfalls into opportunities for profound personal growth and self-discovery. To support you in integrating these teachings and applying them to your own unique context, take a moment to pause and reflect on the following questions. Approach your reflections with openness, curiosity, and self-compassion, and trust that your honest engagement with these prompts will guide you toward a more empowered and authentic relationship with yourself and the world around you.

1. Reflect on your current self-care practices and how your busy schedule might be impacting your ability to prioritize your own needs and well-being. What are one or two small, manageable changes you could make to your daily routine to create more space for self-care and self-love?

2. Consider your relationship with social media and how it may be influencing your sense of self-worth and authenticity. What patterns or habits do you notice in your online engagement that leave you feeling drained, inadequate, or disconnected from your true self? What boundaries or intentional practices could you put in place to cultivate a more positive and empowering digital presence?

3. Take a moment to assess your current financial habits and beliefs. How do your spending patterns and money mindset align with your core values and self-love goals? What fears, doubts, or limiting beliefs arise when you consider making changes to your financial lifestyle?

4. Identify one technological tool or resource that you feel drawn to exploring as a support for your self-love journey. What specifically appeals to you about this tool, and how do you envision it enhancing your self-care practices or personal growth? What reservations or concerns, if any, do you have about incorporating this tool into your life?

5. Imagine yourself fully embracing self-love in the modern world, with a balanced and intentional relationship to technology, social media, and financial well-being. What does this version of yourself look like? How does she feel in her mind, body, and spirit? What new possibilities open up for her when she is grounded in authentic self-love and self-respect?

6. Reflect on the role of community and connection in your self-love journey. How can you cultivate supportive and uplifting relationships, both online and off, that inspire you to show up as your most authentic and empowered self? What qualities or values do you want to prioritize in your interactions and collaborations with others?

Remember, the journey of self-love in the modern world is an ongoing and ever-evolving process. It requires patience, self-compassion, and a willingness to experiment and adapt as you discover what works best for you. Be gentle with yourself as you navigate the ups and downs, and celebrate every small victory along the way. Trust that by staying true to your own inner wisdom and continually choosing yourself, you are creating a ripple effect of positive change that extends far beyond your own life. Keep shining your light, speaking your truth, and embracing your most authentic and love-filled self—the world needs your unique magic now more than ever.

Chapter 5:

Cultivating a Self-Love Lifestyle

We've made it to the final chapter of our self-love journey. Can you believe it? We've covered so much ground together—from breaking down the barriers to self-love to exploring the unique challenges and opportunities of practicing self-love in the modern world.

However, self-love is not just a destination to be reached but a lifelong practice to be cultivated. It is about creating a lifestyle that supports your overall well-being, happiness, and fulfillment—not just in the big, momentous occasions but in the small, everyday moments that make up the fabric of your life.

In this chapter, we're going to explore what it means to cultivate a self-love lifestyle. We'll talk about living authentically and building resilience, pursuing joy and fulfillment, and practicing self-love in your relationships with others. At the end of the day, self-love is not just about how you treat yourself—it is about how you show up in the world and interact with those around you.

So, let's dive in, shall we? Let's explore what it means to create a life that is truly aligned with your values, passions, and authentic self. Because that, my friends, is the ultimate expression of self-love.

Living Authentically and Building Resilience

What does it mean to live authentically, and why is it so important for self-love and well-being?

At its core, authenticity is about being true to yourself—your values, beliefs, desires, and unique personality and quirks. It is about showing up in the world as your full, genuine self without apology or compromise.

In a world that often rewards conformity and people-pleasing, living authentically can be easier said than done. We might feel pressure to fit in, to be liked, to avoid rocking the boat or making waves. We might have internalized messages from family, society, or culture about who we "should" be or how we "should" behave.

When we constantly suppress or hide parts of ourselves to please others or fit in, we pay a high price. We might feel disconnected from our true selves, unfulfilled in our relationships and pursuits, or like we're constantly wearing a mask or playing a role.

That is why living authentically is so important for self-love and well-being. When we embrace our true selves and show up in the world as we really are, we create a sense of inner peace, wholeness, and alignment. We attract people and experiences that resonate with our authentic selves, and we feel more confident, empowered, and resilient in the face of challenges or setbacks.

How can you start living more authentically in your own life? Here are a few tips:

- Get clear on your values and priorities. What matters most to you in life? What kind of person do you want to be? What legacy do you want to leave behind? When you have a strong sense of your values and priorities, making decisions and taking actions that align with your authentic self becomes easier.

- Practice self-awareness and self-reflection. Take time to check in with yourself regularly—your thoughts, feelings, desires, and intuition. Notice when you feel most alive, fulfilled, and true to yourself and when you feel disconnected, drained, or out of alignment. Use this awareness to guide your choices and actions.

- Embrace your unique strengths, quirks, and imperfections. Instead of trying to fit into someone else's mold or ideal, celebrate what makes you different and special. Own your story, your struggles, and your triumphs. Remember that your worth and value come from within, not from external validation or approval.

- Set boundaries and learn to say no. Living authentically means being selective about where you invest your time, energy, and attention. It means saying no to things that don't align with your values or priorities, even if it disappoints others or goes against social norms. Remember, you are not responsible for managing other people's emotions or expectations. Your first responsibility is to yourself and your own well-being.

- Surround yourself with people who support and celebrate your authentic self. Seek out relationships and communities that allow you to be fully yourself without judgment or pressure to conform. Let go of toxic or draining relationships that don't serve your highest good. You deserve to be loved and accepted for who you truly are.

Living authentically is a lifelong practice, and it is not always easy. There will be times when you feel scared, vulnerable, or uncertain. There will be times when you face criticism, rejection, or disapproval from others.

The beautiful thing is that the more you practice living authentically, the more resilient you become. When you have a strong sense of self and a deep connection to your own truth, you become better equipped to handle the ups and downs of life with grace, courage, and compassion.

You learn to trust yourself and your own inner wisdom, even in the face of external challenges or setbacks. You learn to bounce back from disappointments and failures, knowing that they do not define your worth or value as a person. You learn to find strength and purpose in your own unique journey, even when it looks different from everyone else's.

Most importantly, you learn to love and accept yourself fully—not just the polished, perfect parts but also the messy, imperfect, and beautifully human parts. Because that, my friends, is the essence of self-love and the foundation of a truly authentic and fulfilling life.

Cultivating Joy and Fulfillment

Alright, let's talk about joy. And I'm not just talking about the fleeting, superficial kind of happiness that comes from external validation or material possessions. I'm talking about the deep, soul-level joy that comes from living a life that is truly aligned with your values, passions, and purpose.

Too often, we get caught up in the daily grind of work, responsibilities, and obligations, and we forget to make time for the things that truly light us up and bring us alive. We might tell ourselves that we'll pursue our passions and interests "someday" when we have more time, money, or energy. But the truth is, "someday" is not guaranteed—the only time we have is now.

That is why cultivating joy and fulfillment is such an important part of a self-love lifestyle. When we make time for the things that bring us genuine happiness and satisfaction, we create a sense of meaning, purpose, and vitality in our lives. We feel more energized, inspired, and connected to ourselves and the world around us.

So, how can you start cultivating more joy and fulfillment in your life? Here are a few ideas:

- Identify your passions and interests. What activities or pursuits make you lose track of time, light you up from the inside out, or give you a sense of flow and absorption? Maybe it is painting, writing, dancing, hiking, cooking, or volunteering for a cause you care about. Make a list of the things that bring you joy and fulfillment, and commit to incorporating them into your life on a regular basis.

- Practice gratitude and appreciation. Take time each day to reflect on the things you are thankful for - big and small. Maybe it is a supportive friend, a beautiful sunset, a cozy cup of tea, or a small victory at work. When we focus on the good in our lives, we train our brains to look for more of it, and we cultivate a sense of abundance and positivity.

- Engage in acts of kindness and generosity. One of the quickest ways to boost our own happiness and fulfillment is to make someone else's day a little brighter. Look for opportunities to perform random acts of kindness, whether it is giving a genuine compliment, helping a neighbor with a task, or donating to a cause you care about. When we give to others, we also give to ourselves.

- Embrace creativity and playfulness. As adults, we often lose touch with our innate sense of creativity and wonder. However, engaging in creative pursuits and playful activities can be a powerful way to tap into our joy and vitality. Try taking an art class, joining a sports league, or hosting a game night with friends. Remember, it is not about the end result—it is about the process of letting loose, having fun, and expressing yourself freely.

- Cultivate mindfulness and presence. So much of our stress and dissatisfaction comes from dwelling on the past or worrying about the future. When we learn to be fully present in the moment, we open ourselves up to the joy and beauty that is available to us right here, right now. Try incorporating mindfulness practices like meditation, deep breathing, or yoga into your daily routine. Or simply take a few moments throughout the day to pause, notice your surroundings, and savor the small pleasures of life.

Remember, cultivating joy and fulfillment is not about chasing some elusive state of constant happiness or bliss. It is about creating a life that is rich in meaning, purpose, and authentic expression. It is about finding the beauty and wonder in the ordinary moments and savoring the journey as much as the destination.

Most importantly, it is about giving yourself permission to prioritize your own happiness and well-being, even in the face of external pressures or expectations. Because when you fill your own cup first, you have so much more to give to others and the world around you.

So, go ahead, my friends. Pursue those passions, practice those gratitudes, and embrace that playful spirit. Your joy and fulfillment are not a luxury; they are a necessity for a life well-lived.

Self-Love in Relationships

We've talked about living authentically and cultivating joy and fulfillment in your own life. But here's the thing: self-love doesn't exist in a vacuum. It also plays a crucial role in how we show up in our relationships with others—whether that is with romantic partners, family members, friends, or colleagues.

When we have a strong foundation of self-love and self-respect, we are better equipped to create healthy, fulfilling, and mutually supportive relationships with others. We know our own worth and value, and we are less likely to settle for relationships that don't honor or respect us. We are more able to set clear boundaries, communicate our needs and desires, and navigate conflicts with compassion and integrity.

On the other hand, when we lack self-love and self-respect, we are more likely to engage in unhealthy or toxic relationship patterns. We might find ourselves constantly seeking external validation and approval, compromising our own values and needs to please others, or staying in relationships that are unfulfilling or even abusive.

That is why practicing self-love in relationships is so important. It allows us to show up as our best selves, create relationships based on mutual respect, trust, and support, and experience the deep joy and intimacy that comes from authentic connection with others.

How can you start practicing self-love in your relationships? Here are a few tips:

- Set clear boundaries and communicate your needs. Know your own limits and values, and be willing to communicate them clearly and assertively to others. Remember, setting boundaries is not selfish; it is a necessary act of self-care and self-respect. When you honor your needs and desires, you create space for others to do the same.

- Practice self-compassion and self-forgiveness. No one is perfect, and relationships can be messy and complicated. When conflicts or challenges arise, be kind and understanding with yourself. Acknowledge your humanity and imperfections, and extend the same grace and compassion to others. Remember, forgiveness is not about condoning hurtful behavior; it is about releasing the pain and resentment that can hold you back from healing and growth.

- Cultivate self-awareness and emotional intelligence. Pay attention to your thoughts, feelings, and reactions in relationships. Notice when you feel triggered, defensive, or reactive and take responsibility for your emotional responses. Practice active listening, empathy, and non-violent communication. Remember, the goal is not to be right or to win—it is to understand and connect with others on a deeper level.

- Surround yourself with supportive and uplifting relationships. Seek out relationships that allow you to be your authentic self, challenge you to grow and evolve, and bring out the best in you. Let go of relationships that drain your energy, undermine your self-worth, or hold you back from your highest potential.

Remember, you deserve to be loved and supported for who you truly are.

- Practice self-love and self-care in your relationships. Make time for your own needs and priorities, even in the context of your relationships. Continue to pursue your passions, interests, and goals, and encourage your loved ones to do the same. Remember, the healthiest relationships are those in which both partners are able to maintain their own sense of individuality and autonomy while also supporting and uplifting each other.

Practicing self-love in relationships is a lifelong journey, and it is not always easy. There will be times when you feel vulnerable, uncertain, or afraid. There will be times when you face conflicts, misunderstandings, or disappointments with others.

Here's the beautiful thing: When you have a strong foundation of self-love and self-respect, you have the resilience and courage to navigate these challenges with grace and wisdom. You trust yourself to make choices that align with your values and needs, even when they are difficult or uncomfortable. You know that your worth and value are not dependent on the approval or acceptance of others but on your own inherent worthiness and dignity.

Most importantly, you experience the deep joy and fulfillment that comes from creating relationships based on mutual respect, trust, and authentic connection. You experience the beauty and richness of life that comes from showing up fully as yourself and allowing others to do the same.

Practice self-love in your relationships, and watch as they blossom and thrive in ways you never thought possible. Remember, the love and respect you show yourself is the foundation for the love and respect you can give and receive from others.

Finding Meaning and Purpose in Self-Love

As you deepen your commitment to self-love and create a lifestyle that supports your well-being and authenticity, you may find yourself naturally drawn to questions of meaning and purpose. After all, when we learn to love and honor ourselves fully, we often feel called to explore how we can use our unique gifts and passions to make a positive impact on the world around us.

Finding meaning and purpose through self-love is not about achieving some external goal or milestone but about aligning our daily actions and choices with our deepest values and desires. It is about asking ourselves, "What lights me up from the inside out? What kind of life do I want to create for myself and others? How can I use my unique strengths and experiences to contribute to something greater than myself?"

One powerful way to explore these questions is through the practice of self-reflection and journaling. Set aside time each day, or even just once a week, to check in with yourself and explore what feels most meaningful and fulfilling to you in this moment. You might ask yourself questions like, "When do I feel most alive and engaged? What challenges or issues in the world tug at my heartstrings? What legacy do I want to leave behind?"

As you reflect on these questions, pay attention to any themes, insights, or ideas that emerge. You may start to notice patterns in the kinds of experiences or pursuits that bring you the greatest sense of purpose and fulfillment. You may also identify areas of your life where you feel disconnected or unfulfilled and start brainstorming ways to align your choices and actions more fully with your values.

Another way to find meaning and purpose through self-love is to actively seek out opportunities to use your gifts and passions in service of others. This might mean volunteering for a cause you care about, sharing your skills and knowledge with others through teaching or mentoring, or simply showing up as a compassionate and supportive presence for loved ones going through a tough time.

Remember, finding meaning and purpose is not about having it all figured out or achieving some grand, world-changing goal. It is about staying curious and open to the invitations and opportunities that arise when we love and honor ourselves fully. It is about trusting that by showing up as our most authentic and radiant selves, we naturally create a ripple effect of positivity and inspiration in the world around us.

As you continue on your self-love journey, keep exploring what feels most meaningful and fulfilling to you. Keep asking yourself how you can use your unique gifts and experiences to make a positive impact, no matter how small or large. And trust that by aligning your daily actions and choices with your deepest values and desires, you are not only creating a life of profound meaning and purpose for yourself but also contributing to the healing and transformation of the world around you.

Self-Love as a Lifelong Practice

As we come to the end of this exploration of self-love, it is important to remember that cultivating a self-love lifestyle is not a one-time achievement or destination but a lifelong practice and commitment. Just like any other skill or habit, self-love requires ongoing attention, effort, and dedication to truly integrate into our daily lives and relationships.

There will be moments on your self-love journey when you feel like you're soaring high, fully embodying your authentic self and radiating joy and purpose in every area of your life. And there will be other moments when you feel like you've taken two steps back, falling into old patterns of self-doubt, self-criticism, or people-pleasing.

Both experiences are natural and essential parts of the self-love journey. The key is to approach each moment with compassion, curiosity, and a willingness to keep showing up for yourself, no matter what. Remember that growth is not always linear and that even the most challenging moments can be opportunities for deeper self-awareness, healing, and transformation.

One way to support yourself in making self-love a lifelong practice is to surround yourself with reminders, resources, and communities that inspire and uplift you on your journey. This might mean filling your space with affirmations, quotes, or images that remind you of your inherent worth and value. It might mean regularly connecting with friends, mentors, or support groups who share your commitment to self-love and personal growth. Or it might mean continuing to educate yourself and explore new practices and perspectives that expand your capacity for self-love and self-discovery.

Another key to making self-love a lifelong practice is to approach it with a spirit of self-compassion and patience. You must recognize that there will be days when your inner critic is louder than your inner cheerleader and meet those moments with kindness and understanding rather than judgment or frustration. You must celebrate your progress and victories, no matter how small, and trust that every step you take towards loving yourself more fully is planting seeds for a lifetime of growth and transformation.

Ultimately, the invitation of self-love is not to achieve some perfect, unblemished state of being but to embrace the fullness of our humanity—the light and the shadow, the joys and the sorrows, the triumphs and the challenges, to learn to love and accept ourselves in all of our beautiful complexity and extend that same love and acceptance to others as we navigate the ups and downs of life together.

As you continue on this lifelong journey of self-love, remember to be patient and compassionate with yourself. Remember that you are worth the effort and dedication it takes to show up for yourself each day and that every moment of self-love and self-care is an investment in your healing, growth, and happiness.

Know that no matter where you are on your self-love journey, you are never alone. You are part of a global community of individuals who are awakening to their own inherent worth and embracing a life of radical self-love and authenticity. By showing up for yourself each day and shining your light more brightly, you inspire others to do the same and contribute to a world where all beings can thrive and love themselves fully.

So, keep going, keep growing, and keep loving yourself fiercely and unapologetically. The journey of self-love is not always easy, but it is always, always worth it. With each step you take, you are creating a ripple effect of love, healing, and transformation that extends far beyond yourself to others and to the world. Thank yourself for the courage, compassion, and commitment you have shown throughout this journey. Know that you are enough, exactly as you are and that the world needs your unique magic now more than ever. Keep shining, keep growing, and keep loving yourself fiercely and unapologetically—the best is yet to come.

Putting It All Together

We've explored the barriers to self-love and how to overcome them with compassion and resilience. We've navigated the challenges of practicing self-love in the modern world, from the pressures of social media to the demands of a busy lifestyle. We've cultivated a self-love lifestyle that encompasses living authentically, pursuing joy and fulfillment, and creating healthy and supportive relationships with others.

This is just the beginning. Self-love is not a destination to be reached but a lifelong practice to be cultivated and nurtured. It is a journey of self-discovery, self-acceptance, and self-empowerment that will continue to unfold and evolve throughout your life.

As you move forward on this journey, remember the key lessons and strategies we've explored together. Remember to treat yourself with kindness, compassion, and respect, even in the face of challenges or setbacks. Remember to prioritize your own needs and desires and to set clear boundaries with others. Remember to pursue your passions and interests and to find joy and fulfillment in the present moment. Remember to surround yourself with people and experiences that uplift and inspire you and allow you to be your most authentic and radiant self.

Most importantly, remember that you are worthy of love and belonging, just as you are. You are enough, exactly as you are, in this moment and in every moment. Your worth and value are not dependent on your achievements, appearance, relationship status, or any external measure of success. They are inherent in your very being, and they can never be taken away from you.

So, go forth, my dear friends, and live a life of self-love and self-empowerment. Embrace your authentic self and let your unique light shine brightly in the world. Pursue your dreams and passions with courage and determination and trust in your own resilience and strength. Love yourself fiercely and unapologetically, knowing that you are deserving of all the love, joy, and abundance that life has to offer.

Remember, this journey of self-love is not always easy, but it is always worth it. There will be ups and downs, triumphs and challenges, moments of clarity, and moments of confusion. Through it all, know that you are never alone. You have the love and support of a community of fellow travelers, all on their own unique paths of self-discovery and self-empowerment.

Keep going, my dear friends. Keep showing up for yourself, day after day, with patience, compassion, and grace. Keep learning, growing, and evolving, and trust in the wisdom and guidance of your own inner voice. And most importantly, keep believing in yourself and your inherent worthiness and beauty.

The world needs your light, love, and unique gifts. The world needs you to show up fully as yourself and to inspire others to do the same. When you do, you create a ripple effect of love and positivity that touches everyone and everything around you.

Case Study: Embracing a Self-Love Lifestyle

Meet Lila, a 38-year-old high school teacher who had always put others' needs before her own. Lila rarely said no to others' requests, whether it was staying late to help a struggling student, taking on extra committee work, or canceling her own plans to babysit for a friend. While she found joy in helping others, Lila often felt drained, unfulfilled, and disconnected from her own desires and passions.

One summer, Lila reached a breaking point. Exhausted from the demands of the school year and feeling like she had lost touch with herself, Lila knew something needed to change. She decided to take a solo trip to a quiet beach town, hoping to reconnect with herself and rediscover what brought her joy.

During her trip, Lila began to practice self-love in small but meaningful ways. She started each day with a gentle yoga practice and a nourishing breakfast, savoring the peaceful moments to herself. She explored the local art galleries and bookstores, allowing herself to get lost in her own curiosity and interests. And she set boundaries with loved ones back home, letting them know that this time was for her own rest and renewal.

As Lila began to prioritize her own needs and desires, she felt a profound shift within herself. She realized that her own joy and fulfillment were not selfish or frivolous but essential to her overall well-being and ability to show up fully in her life and relationships.

Inspired by her transformative trip, Lila began to cultivate a self-love lifestyle back home. She started setting clearer boundaries at work, learning to say no to extra demands that drained her energy. She carved out time each week for her favorite hobbies, like painting and hiking, and joined a local book club to connect with others who shared her love of literature.

Lila also began to practice self-love in her relationships, communicating her needs and desires more assertively while also holding space for others to do the same. She found that the more she honored her own authenticity and boundaries, the more her relationships flourished with mutual respect, compassion, and understanding.

Of course, embracing a self-love lifestyle was not always easy for Lila. There were times when old patterns of people-pleasing and self-neglect resurfaced and moments when she doubted her own worth and value. But through it all, Lila remained committed to her own growth and healing, knowing that true self-love was a lifelong practice.

As Lila continued to prioritize her own joy, fulfillment, and authentic expression, she noticed a ripple effect in her life and community. Her students and colleagues commented on her renewed energy and passion in the classroom, and her friends and family celebrated the positive changes they saw in her.

Most importantly, Lila felt a deep sense of peace, purpose, and empowerment within herself. She knew that by loving and honoring herself fully, she was not only creating a more vibrant and fulfilling life for herself but also modeling the power of self-love for others.

Through her journey, Lila discovered that a self-love lifestyle is not a one-time achievement but a daily practice of choosing herself, again and again. It is about living authentically, pursuing joy and fulfillment, and cultivating healthy and nourishing relationships—both with others and with oneself.

By embracing a self-love lifestyle, Lila learned to trust her own inner wisdom, celebrate her own quirks and imperfections, and show up fully and unapologetically as herself in the world. In doing so, she discovered the true essence of a life well-lived.

Exercise 1: Crafting a Self-Love Manifesto

1. Take some time to reflect on your core values, beliefs, and desires. What matters most to you in life? What kind of person do you want to be? What brings you joy and fulfillment?

2. Based on your reflections, write a self-love manifesto—a declaration of your commitment to loving, honoring, and caring for yourself. Your manifesto can be as long or short as you like, but aim for at least 10 powerful statements or affirmations.

3. Start each statement with a strong, positive affirmation, such as "I am..." or "I choose..." or "I deserve..." For example: "I am worthy of love and respect, just as I am," or "I choose to

prioritize my own joy and well-being," or "I deserve to live a life that feels authentic and fulfilling to me."

4. Use empowering and uplifting language throughout your manifesto. Focus on what you want to cultivate and embody rather than what you want to avoid or eliminate.

5. Include statements that reflect your commitment to living authentically, pursuing your passions, setting healthy boundaries, practicing self-compassion, and cultivating nourishing relationships.

6. Once you have written your manifesto, read it out loud to yourself, feeling the power and truth of each statement. Make any revisions or additions that feel aligned with your heart.

7. Create a beautiful visual representation of your manifesto. You might hand-letter it, create a collage, or design a digital graphic. Display your manifesto somewhere you will see it often as a daily reminder of your commitment to self-love.

8. Revisit your manifesto regularly, especially in moments when you feel disconnected from your own worth and value. Let it be a source of inspiration, encouragement, and grounding in your ongoing self-love practice.

The goal of this exercise is to clarify and articulate your commitment to a self-love lifestyle. By crafting a powerful and personalized manifesto, you are setting a clear intention for how you want to show up for yourself and in the world. Your manifesto can serve as a north star, guiding you back to your truth and purpose whenever you feel lost or uncertain on your self-love journey.

Exercise 2: Cultivating Joy and Fulfillment Through a Self-Date

1. Schedule a date with yourself—a dedicated block of time (at least 2–3 hours) to focus solely on your own joy, pleasure, and fulfillment. Treat this self-date with the same commitment and excitement you would a date with a loved one.

2. Reflect on what activities, experiences, or environments make you come alive and light you up from the inside out. What have you been longing to do, see, or explore? What nourishes your mind, body, and soul?

3. Based on your reflections, plan a self-date that aligns with your authentic desires and interests. Your date might involve exploring a new neighborhood, taking a dance class, attending a poetry reading, trying a new recipe, or simply savoring a delicious meal in your favorite park.

4. On the day of your self-date, set a clear intention to be fully present and attentive to your own needs, desires, and experiences. Silence your phone, let go of any outside obligations or distractions, and give yourself permission to immerse yourself in the moment.

5. Throughout your self-date, practice mindfulness and self-compassion. Notice any self-critical thoughts or judgments that arise, and gently redirect your attention back to the present moment. Savor the sensations, emotions, and insights that emerge without attaching to or analyzing them.

6. Allow yourself to be spontaneous, playful, and curious. Follow your intuition and let your self-date unfold organically, even if it deviates from your original plan. Embrace the joy and aliveness of being fully present with yourself.

7. After your self-date, take some time to reflect on the experience. What did you learn about yourself and your own needs and desires? What moments of joy, peace, or fulfillment stood out to you? How can you incorporate more of these experiences into your daily life?

8. Commit to making self-dates a regular part of your self-love practice, whether it is weekly, monthly, or quarterly. Remember that prioritizing your own joy and fulfillment is not selfish or frivolous but an essential part of living a vibrant and authentic life.

The goal of this exercise is to cultivate a deeper relationship with yourself and your needs and desires. By regularly taking yourself on self-dates, you are sending a powerful message that your own joy and fulfillment matter. You are creating space to explore your passions, interests, and curiosities and savor the richness and beauty of your inner world. Through this practice, you may discover new aspects of yourself and your own aliveness and integrate more moments of joy and presence into your daily life.

Self-Reflection Questions

As you come to the end of this transformative journey into self-love, take a moment to pause and reflect on how far you've come. From understanding the fundamentals of self-love to overcoming barriers, navigating the modern world, and now cultivating a lifestyle that embodies self-love in every aspect of your being, you have grown and evolved in ways that may have once seemed unimaginable. You've faced challenges, confronted old patterns and beliefs, and emerged with a deeper sense of your own inherent worthiness and value. And while the path of self-love is a lifelong journey, with ups and downs and twists and turns along the way, you now have the tools, insights, and resilience to meet whatever lies ahead with grace, compassion, and unwavering commitment to your own well-being.

As you integrate the lessons and practices from this final chapter into your daily life, remember that cultivating a self-love lifestyle is not about perfection or reaching some ultimate destination. It is about showing up for yourself, again and again, in small moments and big choices, and aligning your thoughts, words, and actions with your deepest values and desires. It is about embracing your authentic self, celebrating your unique gifts and quirks, and building the resilience to weather life's storms with self-compassion and trust in your own strength. It is about creating a life that is rich in joy, purpose, and meaningful connection—both with yourself and with others who support and uplift you on your path.

To support you in reflecting on this chapter and setting intentions for your self-love lifestyle moving forward, consider exploring the following questions, either on your own or with a trusted friend or journal. Remember, there are no right or wrong answers, only the opportunity to deepen your self-awareness and recommit to your growth and happiness.

1. Reflect on a time when you felt most fully and authentically yourself. What circumstances and factors allowed you to show up in this way? How can you create more moments of authentic self-expression and alignment in your daily life?

2. What are some of the masks or personas you find yourself wearing in different areas of your life, whether at work, in relationships, or in social situations? What would it look like to start shedding these masks and showing up more fully as your true self, even if it feels vulnerable or uncomfortable at first?

3. Identify the top three values or priorities that bring you the greatest sense of joy, fulfillment, and purpose. How can you start orienting your time, energy, and resources towards these values and letting go of activities or commitments that drain you or feel misaligned?

4. Reflect on your current relationships and the ways in which they support or hinder your self-love practice. Are there any boundaries you need to set, conversations you need to have, or shifts you need to make to cultivate more nourishing and uplifting connections? What qualities do you want to embody more fully in your relationships with others?

5. Imagine yourself one year from now, living a life that fully embodies self-love and authentic expression. What does your daily routine look like? How do you spend your time and energy? What kind of people and experiences do you surround yourself with? How does it feel to be this version of yourself?

6. What practices or rituals can you put in place to stay connected to your self-love journey and cultivate more joy, resilience, and purpose in your daily life? Consider things like regular self-dates, creative pursuits, mindfulness practices, or connecting with a supportive community.

Remember, the journey of self-love is not a linear path but a spiral of growth and evolution. There will be moments of doubt, resistance, and falling back into old patterns; this is a natural part of the process. What matters is that you keep coming back to yourself, recommitting to your own worth and well-being, and surrounding yourself with people and practices that support your highest self.

As you move forward from here, know that you are not alone on this path. You are part of a rising tide of individuals who are awakening to their own inherent worthiness and embracing a life of radical self-love and authenticity. By claiming your place in this movement and shining your light more brightly each day, you inspire others to do the same and create a ripple effect of healing and transformation that extends far beyond your personal journey.

Take a deep breath, place a hand on your heart, and whisper a silent thank you to yourself for the courage, compassion, and commitment you have shown throughout this journey. Know that you are enough, exactly as you are, and that the world needs your unique magic now more than ever. Keep shining, keep growing, and keep loving yourself fiercely and unapologetically—the best is yet to come.

If You Liked This Book, You Might Also Like...

Conclusion

We've explored the barriers to self-love and how to overcome them with compassion and resilience. We've navigated the challenges of practicing self-love in the modern world, from the pressures of social media to the demands of a busy lifestyle. We've cultivated a self-love lifestyle that encompasses living authentically, pursuing joy and fulfillment, and creating healthy and supportive relationships—both with others and with ourselves.

This, however, is just the beginning. Self-love is not a destination to be reached but a lifelong practice to be cultivated and nurtured. It is a journey of self-discovery, self-acceptance, and self-empowerment that will continue to unfold and evolve throughout your life.

As you move forward on this journey, remember the key lessons and strategies we've explored together. Remember to treat yourself with kindness, compassion, and respect, even in the face of challenges or setbacks. Remember to prioritize your own needs and desires and set clear boundaries with others. Remember to pursue your passions and interests and find joy and fulfillment in the present moment. Remember to surround yourself with people and experiences that uplift and inspire you and allow you to be your most authentic and radiant self.

Most importantly, remember that you are worthy of love and belonging, just as you are. Your worth and value are not contingent on your achievements, appearance, relationship status, or any external measure of success. They are inherent in your very being and can never be taken away from you.

So, go forth, my dear friends, and live a life of unapologetic self-love. Embrace your authentic self, quirks and all, and let your unique light shine brightly in the world. Pursue your dreams and passions with courage and determination, trusting in your resilience and strength. Love yourself fiercely and completely, knowing that you are deserving of all the joy, fulfillment, and abundance that life has to offer.

This journey of self-love is not always easy, but it is always worth it. There will be ups and downs, triumphs and challenges, moments of clarity, and moments of confusion. But through it all, know that you are never alone. You have the love and support of a community of fellow travelers, all on their own unique paths of self-discovery and self-empowerment.

Keep going, my dear friends. Keep showing up for yourself, day after day, with patience, compassion, and grace. Keep learning, growing, and evolving, trusting in the wisdom and guidance of your inner voice. Keep believing in yourself and your inherent beauty and worthiness.

As we close the pages of this book, I want to leave you with a few final thoughts and reflections. First, know that the journey of self-love is not a linear one. There will be days when you feel like you're making great strides and others when you feel like you're taking two steps back. That is okay. Progress is not always a straight line, and setbacks are a natural part of the process. What matters is that you keep coming back to yourself, again and again, with love and compassion.

Second, remember that self-love is not about perfection. It is not about never making mistakes, never feeling insecure, or never struggling. It is about learning to embrace and love all parts of yourself—the light and the dark, the beautiful and the messy. It is about extending yourself the same grace and understanding that you would offer a dear friend and treating yourself with the utmost kindness and respect, even on your most difficult days.

Finally, know that by cultivating a deep and unshakable love for yourself, you are not only transforming your own life but also contributing to the healing and transformation of the world around you. When you show up in the world as your most authentic, radiant, and empowered self, you inspire others to do the same. You create a ripple effect of love, compassion, and positive change that touches everyone and everything in its wake.

As you close this book and step forward into the next chapter of your self-love journey, do so with courage, conviction, and an open heart. Trust in the power of your inner wisdom and resilience and know that you have everything you need to create a life of profound meaning, joy, and fulfillment.

Above all else, remember this: You are worth it. You are worth the time, energy, and effort it takes to cultivate a deep and lasting love for yourself. You are worth the uncomfortable conversations, the moments of vulnerability, and the leaps of faith. You are worth investing in, believing in, and fighting for.

Because when you truly love and accept yourself, anything is possible. You become unstoppable, unshakeable, and capable of creating the life of your dreams. You step into your power and your purpose, and you begin to live in alignment with your deepest values and desires.

So, here's to you, my dear friends. Here's to your courage, your resilience, and your unwavering commitment to self-love and self-discovery. Here's to the beautiful, messy, unpredictable journey ahead of you and to all the magic and miracles that await you along the way.

I want you to know that your feedback will be instrumental in shaping the insights, tools, and practices we explore as we bring our journey to a close. I believe that the conclusion of this book should not be an ending but a beginning—a launching pad for you to take the lessons and insights you've gained and put them into action in your own life in your own unique way. If you could be so kind as to leave a review, your feedback will impact others and shape the next steps of the book's journey.

Scan QR code to LEAVE A REVIEW

References

Ben-Ze'ev, A. (2019). Is self-fulfillment essential for romantic love? The self-other tension in romantic love. *Revista de Filosofia Aurora*, *31*(54). https://doi.org/10.7213/1980-5934.31.054.ds12

Brown, B. (2013). Daring Greatly. Penguin UK.

Chazan, P. (1998). Self-esteem, self-respect, and love of self: Ways of valuing the self. *Philosophia*, *26*(1-2), 41–63. https://doi.org/10.1007/bf02380057

Zeigler-Hill, V., Britton, M., Holden, C. J., & Besser, A. (2014). How will I love you? Self-esteem instability moderates the association between self-esteem level and romantic love styles. *Self and Identity*, *14*(1), 118–134. https://doi.org/10.1080/15298868.2014.960445

Printed in Great Britain
by Amazon